BEST

POEMS

ST. ANDREW JUNIOR SCHOOL

Introductory Level

Poems for Young People

with Lessons for Teaching the Basic Elements of Literature

JAMESTOWN PUBLISHERS

a division of NTC/CONTEMPORARY PUBLISHING GROUP
Lincolnwood, Illinois USA

808
BES
AYR-2355

Editorial Development: Patricia Opaskar, Mary Ann Trost
Cover Design: Steve Straus
Cover Illustration: Michael Steirnagle
Interior Design: Steve Straus
Interior Illustrations: Pat Doyle

ISBN: 0-89061-891-7 (hardbound)
ISBN: 0-89061-846-1 (softbound)

Published by Jamestown Publishers,
a division of NTC/Contemporary Publishing Group, Inc.,
4255 West Touhy Avenue,
Lincolnwood (Chicago), Illinois 60712-1975 U.S.A.
© 1998 by NTC/Contemporary Publishing Group, Inc.
All rights reserved. No part of this book may be reproduced,
stored in a retrieval system, or transmitted in any form or by any means,
electronic, mechanical, photocopying, recording, or otherwise,
without prior permission of the publisher.
Manufactured in the United States of America.

5 6 7 8 9 10 11 12 13 14 044 / 055 09 08 07 06 05 04 03

ACKNOWLEDGMENTS

Acknowledgment is gratefully made to the following publishers, authors, and agents for permission to reprint these works. Every effort has been made to determine copyright owners. In the case of any omissions, the Publisher will be pleased to make suitable acknowledgments in future editions.

Acosta, Teresa Palomo. "My Mother Pieced Quilts" by Teresa Palomo Acosta. Reprinted by permission of the author.

Allen, Samuel. "To Satch" by Samuel Allen from *Soon, One Morning*. Reprinted by permission of the author.

Allen, Sara Van Alstyne. "Song for a Surf-Rider" by Sara Van Alstyne Allen from *Instructor*, 1966. Copyright © 1966 by Scholastic Inc. Reprinted by permission of Scholastic, Inc.

Belting, Natalia. "Whirlwind Is a Ghost Dancing" from *Whirlwind is a Ghost Dancing* by Natalia Belting. Copyright © 1974 by Natalia Belting. Used by permission of Dutton Children's Books, a division of Penguin Putnam, Inc.

Benét, Rosemary, and Stephen Vincent Benét. "Western Wagons" from *A Book of Americans* by Rosemary and Stephen Vincent Benét. Holt Rinehart & Winston, Inc. Copyright, 1937 by Stephen Vincent Benét. Copyright renewed © 1964 by Thomas C. Benét: Stephanie B. Mahin: Rachel Lewis Benét. Reprinted by permission of Brandt & Brandt Literary Agents, Inc.

Benét, Rosemary, and Stephen Vincent Benét. "Wilbur Wright and Orville Wright" from *A Book of Americans* by Rosemary and Stephen Vincent Benét. Holt Rinehart & Winston, Inc. Copyright 1933, by Rosemary and Stephen Vincent Benét. Copyright renewed © 1946 by Rosemary Carr Benét. Reprinted by permission of Brandt & Brandt Literary Agents, Inc.

Bonnette, Jeanne DeLamarter. "Vacant House" by Jeanne DeLamarter Bonnette.

Booth, Philip. "Crossing," copyright 1953 by Philip Booth, from *Letter From A Distant Land* by Philip Booth. Used by permission of Viking Penguin, a division of Penguin Putnam, Inc.

Bourinot, Arthur S. "Paul Bunyan" from *Watcher of Men, Selected Poems 1947–1966* by Arthur S. Bourinot. Reprinted by permission of Suzette Bourinot McDonald.

Brooks, Gwendolyn. "We Real Cool" by Gwendolyn Brooks from *Blacks*, Third World Press, Chicago, 1991. © 1991 by Gwendolyn Brooks. Reprinted by permission of the author.

Ciardi, John. "And They Lived Happily Ever After for a While" and "The Shark" from *Fast and Slow* by John Ciardi. Copyright © 1975 by John Ciardi. Reprinted by permission of Houghton Mifflin Co. All rights reserved.

Francis, Robert. "Summons" and "While I Slept" reprinted from *Robert Francis: Collected Poems, 1936-1976* by Robert Francis (Amherst: University of Massachusetts Press, 1976), copyright © 1976 by Robert Francis. Reprinted by permission of the publisher.

Gibson, Wilfrid Wilson. "The Stone" from *The Collected Poems 1905–1925* by Wilfrid Wilson Gibson. Reprinted by permission of Macmillan Publishers Ltd.

Giovanni, Nikki. "Legacies" from *My House* by Nikki Giovanni. Copyright © 1972 by Nikki Giovanni. Reprinted by permission of William Morrow & Company, Inc.

Guiterman, Arthur. "Bears" from *Song and Laughter* by Arthur Guiterman. Reprinted by permission of Louise H. Sclove, for the Estate of Arthur Guiterman.

Guiterman, Arthur. "Dorlan's Home-Walk" from *The Laughing Muse* by Arthur Guiterman. Reprinted by permission of Louise H. Sclove, for the Estate of Arthur Guiterman.

Hay, Sara Henderson. "The Builders" from *Story Hour* by Sara Henderson Hay. Reprinted by permission of The University of Arkansas Press. Copyright 1982 by Sara Henderson Hay.

Hoddinott, Margaret J. "Look at Me" by Margaret J. Hoddinott from *Finding Yourself, Finding Others* by Clark E. Moustakas. Reprinted by permission of the author.

Hughes, Langston. "Daybreak in Alabama" from *Collected Poems* by Langston Hughes. Copyright © 1994 by the Estate of Langston Hughes. Reprinted by permission of Alfred A. Knopf, Inc.

Jeffers, Robinson. "Hands" reprinted from *The Collected Poetry of Robinson Jeffers, Volume Two, 1928–1938*, edited by Tim Hunt, with the permission of the publishers, Stanford University Press. © 1955 by the Board of Trustees of the Leland Stanford Junior University.

Kuskin, Karla. "Write About a Radish" from *Near the Window Tree* by Karla Kuskin. Copyright © 1975 by Karla Kuskin. Reprinted by permission of Scott Treimel New York.

Kyorai, trans. by Harry Behn. Haiku by Kyorai from *More Cricket Songs*. Japanese haiku translated by Harry Behn. Copyright © 1971 Harry Behn. Reprinted by permission of Marian Reiner.

Lee, Li-Young. "I Ask My Mother to Sing" copyright © 1986 by Li-Young Lee. Reprinted from *Rose* with the permission of BOA Editions, Ltd., 260 East Ave., Rochester, NY 14604.

Lindsay, Vachel. "The Flower-fed Buffaloes" from *Going to the Stars* by Vachel Lindsay. Copyright 1926 by D. Appleton & Co., renewed 1954 by Elizabeth C. Lindsay. A Hawthorn Book. Used by permission of Dutton Children's Books, a division of Penguin Putnam, Inc.

Little, Jean. "Oranges" from *Hey World, Here I Am!* by Jean Little. Text copyright © 1986 by Jean Little. Used by permission of HarperCollins Publishers and Kids Can Press, Ltd., Toronto, Canada.

Livingston, Myra Cohn. "Moon" from *Space Songs* by Myra Cohn Livingston (Holiday House). Text Copyright © 1988 by Myra Cohn Livingston. Reprinted by permission of Marian Reiner.

Long, Mary. "An Announcement" by Mary Long. Reprinted by permission of Mary Clare Yates, RSM.

Lueders, Edward. "Your Poem, Man . . ." by Edward Lueders, from *Some Haystacks Don't Even Have Any Needle*. Copyright 1969 by Edward Lueders. Reprinted by permission.

Malanga, Gerard. "Pure Poetry" by Gerard Malanga. © Gerard Malanga. Reprinted by permission.

Masefield, John. "Sea Fever" by John Masefield. Reprinted by permission of The Society of Authors as the Literary Representative of the Estate of John Masefield.

McGinley, Phyllis. "The Giveaway," copyright 1954 by Phyllis McGinley, renewed © 1982 by Phyllis Hayden Blake, from *Times Three* by Phyllis McGinley. Used by permission of Viking Penguin, a division of Penguin Putnam, Inc.

Merriam, Eve. "Argument" from *Out Loud* by Eve Merriam. Text copyright © 1973 by Eve Merriam. Reprinted by permission of Marian Reiner. Drawing by Harriet Sherman; reprinted by permission.

Merriam, Eve. "Like Bookends" from *If Only I Could Tell You* by Eve Merriam. Copyright © 1983 by Eve Merriam. Reprinted by permission of Marian Reiner.

Mtshali, Oswald Mbusyiseni. "Sunset" from *Sounds of a Cowhide Drum* by Oswald Mbuyiseni Mtshali. Published by A. D. Donker, Johannesburg. Reprinted by permission of the publisher.

Murray, Pauli. "Words" from *Dark Testament and Other Poems* by Pauli Murray. Reprinted by permission of Frances Collin, Agent for the Estate of Pauli Murray. Copyright © 1970 by Pauli Murray.

Nelms, Sheryl L. "Cumulus Clouds" by Sheryl L. Nelms; originally appeared in *Modern Maturity*, August–September 1985. Reprinted by permission of the author.

Randall, Dudley. "Ancestors" from *After the Killing* by Dudley Randall. Reprinted by permission of the author.

Reznikoff, Charles. "Poem 11" Copyright © 1977 by Marie Syrkin Reznikoff. Reprinted from *Poems 1918–1975: The Complete Poems of Charles Reznikoff* with the permission of Black Sparrow Press.

Ridlon, Marci. "That Was Summer." Copyright © 1969 by Marci Ridlon and used with permission of the author.

Rivas, Ophelia. "Indians" by Ophelia Rivas. Washington, D.C.: Bureau of Indian Affairs, 1971.

Sarton, May. "Girl with 'Cello'," copyright © 1971 by May Sarton, from *Collected Poems 1930–1993* by May Sarton. Reprinted by permission of W. W. Norton & Company, Inc.

Silverstein, Shel. "Almost Perfect" from *A Light in the Attic* by Shel Silverstein. Copyright © 1981 by Evil Eye Music, Inc. Used by permission of HarperCollins Publishers.

Soseki, trans. by Harry Behn. Haiku by Soseki from *Cricket Songs*. Japanese haiku translated by Harry Behn. Copyright © 1964 Harry Behn. © Renewed 1992 by Prescott Behn, Pamela Behn Adam, and Peter Behn. Reprinted by permission of Marian Reiner.

Soto, Gary. "Oranges" from *New & Selected Poems* by Gary Soto © 1995 published by Chronicle Books, San Francisco. Reprinted by permission of the publisher.

TallMountain, Mary. "There Is No Word for Goodbye" from *There Is No Word for Goodbye* by Mary TallMountain. Copyright © 1994 TallMountain Estate. Reprinted by permission.

Wallace, Robert. "In Winter" by Robert Wallace. © 1968 by Robert Wallace. Reprinted by permission.

Worth, Valerie. "sun" from *Small Poems* by Valerie Worth. Copyright © 1972 by Valerie Worth. Reprinted by permission of Farrar, Straus & Giroux, Inc.

CONTENTS

TO THE STUDENT

People have always been fascinated by words. From cave dwellers of the past to rap artists of today, we have loved the way the sounds and the meanings of words can be combined. Poetry is both an ancient and a modern way of communicating, which combines words, sounds, and images in a special way.

Some critics of modern society say that we live too fast. We speed through life—keeping appointments, making plans, talking and moving quickly—and we hardly ever take the time to reflect upon what is most important. When we read poems, however, we must leave the fast-paced world behind. Poems force us to slow down and think about what we are reading. Because poems are written in an unusual way—in lines that break in strange places and in stanzas instead of paragraphs—they startle us. They encourage us to break away from our usual way of life and to think more deeply. Reading a poem is connecting with another mind in a very personal way, a way that cannot be rushed.

The poems you are about to read give you opportunities to connect with many different minds. Through the poems, you are invited to share jokes, see beautiful or unusual sights, hear exciting or strange stories, meet new people, enjoy rhythms and rhymes, and reflect on important lessons. The special forms in which the poems are written will help you concentrate on what the poets are saying and why they have chosen to say it that way. Take your time as you read these poems. The world can go on without you for a while. Your reward may be finding a particular verse that you will remember and cherish for the rest of your life.

The lessons in this book will help you see how the poets constructed their poems. You will learn about the major elements of poetry and will study the techniques that poets use in their work. You also will have a chance to try some of the techniques in your own writing.

UNIT FORMAT AND ACTIVITIES

- Each unit begins with a list of all the poems you will read in that unit. About the Lessons explains why the poems are grouped the way they are. In general, poems are grouped together because they are particularly good examples of the element of poetry that will be taught in that unit.

- The unit's major writing exercise is then introduced. In this exercise you will begin planning for the writing project that you will complete at the end of the unit. Periodically throughout the unit you will have opportunities to explore and develop ideas for your writing project.

- Next, in As You Read there are questions for you to ask yourself as you read the poems in the unit.

- About This Poet focuses on one particular poet whose work appears in the unit. Here you will learn about the poet's life, major accomplishments, and works.

- The poems themselves make up the next section. Before each poem is a short biography of the poet and/or further information about the poem. These notes have been included because knowing something about a poet and the poem's content may help you better understand and appreciate the work.

- Following the poems are questions that test your comprehension and critical-thinking skills. Your answers to these questions and to other exercises in the unit should be recorded in a personal literature notebook. Check your answers with your teacher.

- Your teacher may provide you with charts to record your progress in developing your comprehension skills: The Comprehension Skills Graph *records* your scores and the Comprehension Skills Profile *analyzes* your scores—providing you with information about the skills on which you need to focus. You can talk with your teacher about ways to work on those comprehension skills.

- The next section contains two or three lessons, which begin with a discussion of the literary concept that is the unit's focus. Each lesson illustrates one or more techniques that poets use to develop the concept. For example, you will see how a poet uses sensory details and concrete language to create memorable images.
- Short-answer exercises test your understanding of the poets' techniques as illustrated in particular poems that appear in the unit. You can check your answers to the exercises with your teacher and determine what you need to review.
- Each lesson also includes a writing exercise that guides you in creating your own original work using the techniques you have just studied.
- Discussion guides and a final writing activity round out each unit in the book. These activities will help sharpen your reading, thinking, speaking, and writing skills.
- At the back of the book is a discussion of the writing process. You may want to refer to it as you complete your writing exercises and projects. You also will find a glossary of literary terms. You can refer to the glossary when you encounter an unfamiliar term or concept.

Reading the poems in this book will enable you to recognize and appreciate the skills it takes to write a good poem. When you understand what makes a poem good, you will be better able to choose and enjoy worthwhile poems on your own. The writing exercises will help you become a better writer by giving you practice in using other poets' techniques to make your own poetry more effective and appealing.

What Is a Poem?

INTRODUCTION

**ABOUT THE
LESSONS**

What makes a poem a poem? Is it the rhyming words? That can't be it, since many poems don't rhyme. Is it the pictures that the words create? It couldn't be only that, since some stories and nonfiction articles are just as descriptive as some poems. Perhaps the rhythm of the words makes poetry different from prose. Certainly some poems have regular rhythms, but not all poems do. So what makes a poem a poem? To a great extent, poetry is a combination of all the above—plus a certain attitude and perspective. The lessons in this unit will focus on the following elements, which are common to most poems: 1) the process of observing, condensing, and sharing an experience; 2) the special forms and sounds of the words; 3) the use of imagery (word pictures), striking comparisons, and exact details. The three groups of poems in this unit will highlight these special elements.

 WRITING: THINKING LIKE A POET

Each of us has a poet inside. If you care deeply about something, if you enjoy the sound of spoken words, and if you notice the world around you, you have what it takes to bring out the poet in you. Throughout this unit you will work with a few classmates to write a group poem. Here are some suggestions to start you thinking like a poet:

- Think about your family, friends, home, school, and neighborhood. How do you feel about each of them? Choose the one group or place about which you have the strongest feelings.
- Make a list of details that describe your chosen group or place. For example, if you have chosen your family, you may list details about the way your parents look and sound

or the way your little brother is always asking you questions. The details on your list may describe what you see, hear, smell, taste, and touch; or they may describe how you feel about your chosen group or place.

- Carry your list with you for at least one day and record any additional details that come to mind.

ABOUT THIS POET

Nikki Giovanni (1943–) was born Yolande Cornelia Giovanni in Knoxville, Tennessee. Although her parents moved to Cincinnati, Ohio, when she was a young child, she spent a great deal of her childhood and teen years with her grandmother in Tennessee. Giovanni graduated with honors from Fisk University, where she was the editor of the school's literary magazine.

While at Fisk, Giovanni became concerned about the problems faced by African Americans, and she worked in organizations whose goals were to revolutionize American society. She expresses her pride in her heritage and her frustration with the poor treatment of her people in her early writing efforts, including *Black Feeling, Black Talk; Black Judgment;* and *Re: Creation.*

In 1969 Giovanni's son Thomas was born. After his birth Giovanni began centering her poetry on the family and on individuals' places in the community, rather than on the political themes that she had focused on previously. Her books *My House* and *The Women and the Men* explore the concerns and delights of being part of a family. Later she produced several books of poetry aimed at young readers, including *Spin a Soft Black Song* and *Vacation Time.*

In 1971 Giovanni recorded an album, *Truth Is on Its Way,* on which she read some of her poems. It became the best-selling spoken-word album of 1971. Its success prompted her to make several other recordings of her own works.

Giovanni has written, taught, and lectured about poetry at colleges and universities for more than 30 years. She is one of the most popular and respected poets of her time and has been given a number of prestigious awards, including election to the Ohio Women's Hall of Fame (1985), the Outstanding Woman of Tennessee award (1985), and the American Library Association's award for Best Books for Young Adults (1973) for *My House*, the book from which the poem "Legacies" has been taken. Throughout her career Giovanni has expressed her feelings as a part of the African-American community, as a parent, and as a member of the human race.

AS YOU READ

As you read each of the poems in this unit, ask yourself these questions. They will help you understand the techniques that the poets used to write their poems.

- Who is the speaker in this poem? What message is the speaker expressing? Which words or lines help me understand the message most clearly? Which words or lines am I having trouble understanding?
- What sounds do I hear in this poem that I don't hear in normal conversation? Does the form of this poem look different from prose?
- What kinds of pictures does this poem create in my mind? How does it affect my feelings?

Summons

by Robert Francis

ABOUT THE SELECTION

Robert Francis (1901–1987) was born in Upland, Pennsylvania. He earned two degrees at Harvard University and was a professional writer of poetry, essays, fiction, and autobiography. His first collection of poetry was published in 1936, and in 1939 he received the first of many awards for his writing. In "Summons" Francis uses a conversational tone that is similar to that in the poetry of his close friend and advisor, poet Robert Frost.

Keep me from going to sleep too soon
Or if I go to sleep too soon
Come wake me up. Come any hour
Of night. Come whistling up the road.
Stomp on the porch. Bang on the door.
Make me get out of bed and come
And let you in and light a light.
Tell me the northern lights[1] are on
And make me look. Or tell me clouds
Are doing something to the moon
They never did before, and show me.
See that I see. Talk to me till
I'm half as wide awake as you
And start to dress wondering why
I ever went to bed at all.
Tell me the walking is superb.
Not only tell me but persuade me.
You know that I'm not too hard persuaded.

---

[1] glowing colored bands or streams of light that sometimes appear in the night sky in the Northern Hemisphere, believed to be electrical discharges in the atmosphere; also called *aurora borealis*

5

An Announcement

by Mary Long

ABOUT THE SELECTION

Newspaper pages and most people's mailboxes are regularly sprinkled with "final notices," announcements of the ends of sales or last chances to take advantage of certain opportunities. Mary Long's poem "An Announcement" applies this familiar approach to an unusual opportunity.

This is your last warning!
If you continue to ignore me,
If you continue to show no interest
     in learning my name,
If you have not spoken a phrase of some sort to
     me
by the end of next week—
I will stop dreaming about you.
The Great American Novel
now being formulated in my head,
of which you are the central character,
will be terminated!
I've given you ample, fair, silent warning.
I await your actions.

Look at Me

by Peg Hoddinott

ABOUT THE SELECTION

"Look at Me" uses the conversational poetry form called *free verse*. Its short lines and simple language avoid any complications that could interfere with its direct message.

Look at me. Please, see me
Not my clothes or stubby nails
Or homely face.
Open your heart, so you can see mine.
I do not ask you to agree with
Or understand all you see
For I don't even do that.
Just look at what is really there
And allow it to be.

Western Wagons

by Rosemary and Stephen Vincent Benét

ABOUT THE SELECTION

Stephen Vincent Benét (1898–1943) was a major American poet and fiction writer whose greatest works focused on important events in American history. He received the Pulitzer Prize for poetry in 1929 for his epic poem about the Civil War, *John Brown's Body*, and again in 1944 for the poem *Western Star,* about the settling of the Plymouth and Jamestown colonies. His wife, Rosemary Carr Benét (1898–1962), was a correspondent for *The London Daily Mail* and the *Chicago Tribune.* In 1933 the couple wrote *A Book of Americans*, a collection of poems about people in American history, including the pioneers who crossed the prairies on their way to the West.

They went with axe and rifle, when the trail was still to
　　blaze,
They went with wife and children, in the prairie-schooner
　　days,
With banjo and with frying pan—Susanna, don't you cry!
For I'm off to California to get rich out there or die!

We've broken land and cleared it, but we're tired of where
　　we are.
They say that wild Nebraska is a better place by far.
There's gold in far Wyoming, there's black earth in Ioway,
So pack up the kids and blankets, for we're moving out
today!

The cowards never started and the weak died on the road,
And all across the continent the endless campfires glowed.
We'd taken land and settled—but a traveler passed by—
And we're going West tomorrow—Lordy, never ask us why!

We're going West tomorrow, where the promises can't fail.
O'er the hills in legions, boys, and crowd the dusty trail!
We shall starve and freeze and suffer. We shall die, and
  tame the lands.
But we're going West tomorrow, with our fortune in our
  hands.

Legacies

by Nikki Giovanni

ABOUT THE SELECTION

In many of her poems, Nikki Giovanni (1943–   ) reflects on her feelings about her family and the joys of family life. Of her writing she has said, "I didn't want to become the kind of writer that was stilted or that used language in ways that could not be spoken." Notice how easy it is to imagine the voices of the girl and her grandmother in the following poem from Giovanni's award-winning book *My House.* For more information about Giovanni, see About This Poet at the beginning of this unit.

her grandmother called her from the playground
       "yes, ma'am"
       "i want chu to learn how to make rolls" said the old
woman proudly
but the little girl didn't want
to learn how because she knew
even if she couldn't say it that
that would mean when the old one died she would be less
dependent on her spirit so
she said
       "i don't want to know how to make no rolls"
with her lips poked out
and the old woman wiped her hands on
her apron saying "lord
       these children"
and neither of them ever
said what they meant
and i guess nobody ever does

Pure Poetry

by Gerard Malanga

ABOUT THE SELECTION

Gerard Malanga (1943–   ) is a prize-winning poet and portrait photographer whose work has been featured in several one-man photographic exhibitions. During the 1960s he was also an actor and assistant director in pop-artist Andy Warhol's films, as well as a dancer with the Velvet Underground rock band. With Warhol, he founded *Interview* magazine and edited the first issues. "Pure Poetry" indicates Malanga's distinctive style of writing.

i keep ~~crossing out words lines whole passages~~
~~until nothing is~~ left
~~except~~ you

Write About
a Radish

by Karla Kuskin

**ABOUT THE
SELECTION**

Karla Kuskin (1932–   ) is both a writer and an illustrator. She began writing poetry as a child, and she wrote and illustrated her first children's book while still a student at Yale University. In addition to poetry and children's books, Kuskin writes screenplays and essays. The following poem is from her 1975 collection, *Dogs & Dragons, Trees & Dreams*.

Write about a radish
Too many people write about the moon.

The night is black
The stars are small and high
The clock unwinds its ever-ticking tune
Hills gleam dimly
Distant nighthawks cry.
A radish rises in the waiting sky.

Your World

by Georgia Douglas Johnson

ABOUT THE SELECTION

Georgia Douglas Johnson (1886–1966) was born in Georgia. She attended Oberlin College and Atlanta University, where she studied literature and music. She lived for many years in Washington, D.C., working as a teacher, a government employee, and a writer. Throughout her life Johnson encouraged other African-American writers in their art. In this poem the speaker draws a comparison between herself and a bird.

Your world is as big as you make it.
I know, for I used to abide
In the narrowest nest in a corner,
My wings pressing close to my side.

But I sighted the distant horizon
where the skyline encircled the sea
And I throbbed with a burning desire
To travel this immensity.

I battered the cordons around me
And cradled my wings on the breeze
Then soared to the uttermost reaches
With rapture, with power, with ease!

Your Poem, Man . . .

by Edward Lueders

ABOUT THE SELECTION

Edward Lueders (1923–) is a poet, essayist, novelist, editor, and teacher who has taught English at colleges and universities in New Mexico, California, Indiana, and Utah. He also has been a jazz pianist. Lueders is best known to teachers and students at the secondary-school level for the poetry anthology he helped to edit called *Reflections on a Gift of Watermelon Pickle* (first edition, 1966; second edition, 1995). He also edited and translated an anthology of modern Japanese poetry, *Like Underground Water* (1995). In "Your Poem, Man . . ." he offers some thoughts on what makes a poem good.

unless there's one thing seen
suddenly against another—a parsnip
sprouting for a President, or
hailstones melting in an ashtray—
nothing really happens. It takes
surprise and wild connections,
doesn't it? A walrus chewing
on a ballpoint pen. Two blue tail-
lights on Tyrannosaurus Rex. Green
cheese teeth. Maybe what we wanted
least. Or most. Some unexpected
pleats. Words that never knew
each other till right now. Plug us
into the wrong socket and see
what blows up—or what lights up.

Try
    untried
        circuitry,[1]
new
    fuses.
Tell it like it never really was,
man,
and maybe we can see it
like it is.

---

[1] system of an electrical circuit or the elements of the circuit

UNDERSTANDING THE POEMS

Record your answers to these questions in your personal literature notebook. Follow the directions for each group.

_____ **GROUP 1**   Reread the poems in Group 1 to complete these sentences.

Reviewing the
Selection

1. The speaker in "Summons" invites someone to come and wake him or her at
   a. sunrise.
   b. any time of day.
   c. sunset.
   d. any time of night.

2. In "Look at Me" the speaker admits all of the following except that he or she
   a. has stubby nails.
   b. understands everything in his or her own heart.
   c. has a homely face.
   d. wants others to accept him or her.

Interpreting the
Selection

3. The speaker in "An Announcement" refers to a "Great American Novel" to signify that he or she
   a. is a famous author working on a new novel.
   b. is addressing a character in a novel.
   c. is addressing someone he or she cares about or admires.
   d. greatly enjoys reading novels.

Recognizing How
Words Are Used

4. "An Announcement" uses the words *formulated, terminated, and await your actions* mostly to
   a. keep children from reading a poem intended for adults.
   b. give it the same tone as an important official notice.
   c. show off the poet's great vocabulary.
   d. take advantage of the pattern of stressed syllables in the words.

Appreciating Poetry

5. The best word to describe the speaker's tone in "Look at Me" is
   a. excited.
   b. fearful.
   c. pleading.
   d. hopeless.

GROUP 2   Reread the poems in Group 2 to complete these sentences.

Reviewing the Selection

6. Standard capitalization and punctuation are used in
   a. "Western Wagons" and "Legacies."
   b. "Western Wagons" and "Pure Poetry."
   c. "Legacies" and "Pure Poetry."
   d. "Western Wagons" only.

7. In "Western Wagons" the endless campfires are said to have glowed
   a. all across North America.
   b. only in Wyoming.
   c. in the state of Ioway.
   d. in California and Nebraska.

Recognizing How Words Are Used

8. In "Western Wagons" the poets say that the settlers went "With banjo and with frying pan." They use these particular words
   a. because frying pans kept the settlers' bodies healthy and banjos kept their spirits healthy.
   b. because banjos and frying pans have similar shapes.
   c. because they wanted to use two words that contain the sound of *an.*
   d. for no particular reason.

*Interpreting the
Selection*

9. The little girl in "Legacies" doesn't want to learn how to make rolls because
   a. her grandmother is a spirit, and she is afraid of spirits.
   b. her grandmother is too proud and difficult to work with.
   c. she feels she is too young to do so much work.
   d. learning to make rolls will make her forget her grandmother after the woman dies.

*Appreciating
Poetry*

10. The main theme, or message, of "Legacies" is that
   a. children never do what their parents and grandparents expect of them.
   b. grandparents are too easily discouraged by uncooperative children.
   c. young girls would rather play than learn to cook.
   d. people find it hard to express what they are really feeling.

GROUP 3

Reread the poems in Group 3 to complete these sentences.

*Reviewing the
Selection*

11. In "Write About a Radish" the speaker is describing
   a. a sunrise.
   b. nighttime.
   c. midday.
   d. a sunset.

12. In "Your World," when the speaker says, "Your world is as big as you make it," he or she means
   a. you control how far you go in life.
   b. your life is governed by circumstances over which you have no control.
   c. you can fool yourself into believing almost anything about the world.
   d. no one has ever figured out exactly how big the world is.

Interpreting the Selection

13. The speaker in "Your Poem, Man . . ." believes that the most important element of poetry is its ability to
a. rhyme in a new way.
b. teach about electricity.
c. surprise the reader.
d. say something in as few words as possible.

Recognizing How Words Are Used

14. In "Your World" words at the ends of these lines rhyme:
a. first and third
b. second and third
c. first and fourth
d. second and fourth

Appreciating Poetry

15. Karla Kuskin wrote "Write About a Radish" because she
a. wanted to write a scary poem.
b. was tired of reading poems about common topics.
c. felt that not enough people write about vegetables.
d. wanted to remind readers that radishes are part of a healthy diet.

Now check your answers with your teacher. Study the questions you answered incorrectly. What types of questions were they? Talk with your teacher about ways to work on those skills.

What Is a Poem?

The *Webster's New World Dictionary* defines a poem as "an arrangement of words written or spoken, traditionally a rhythmical composition, sometimes rhymed, expressing experiences, ideas, or emotions in a style more concentrated, imaginative, and powerful than that of ordinary speech or prose." But what does that mean, and how can readers tell if a piece of writing is good poetry? Lovers and critics of poetry have written libraries full of explanations. This book can only touch on the major elements of poetry to get you started in understanding and appreciating it. The lessons in this unit will give you an overview of poetry and will focus on these points:

- Typically, a poem expresses a highly personal view of an experience or idea in a very compact way. The poet chooses a speaker and a mood to convey the message of the poem in a special way.
- Poems have unique forms and sounds. Poets put their words together in particular ways in order to give flow and form to the lines.
- Poets capture the importance of experiences and ideas by describing them with exact sensory details and by looking at them in new and unusual ways.

LESSON 1 | A POEM IS A PERSONAL EXPRESSION

When writing a novel, an author will use hundreds of pages to tell a story and state important themes. Even when writing a short story or an essay, a writer usually will use several pages to establish a mood, present characters or information, and develop events or ideas. When writing a poem, however, a poet uses just a few lines or stanzas to describe one specific experience or idea. By focusing on just one moment or feeling, the poet is trying to help readers look at an important experience or idea from his or her own unique perspective.

As you read these lines from "Summons," you cannot ignore the passion with which the speaker expresses his or her request:

> Keep me from going to sleep too soon
> Or if I go to sleep too soon
> Come wake me up. Come any hour
> Of night. Come whistling up the road.
> Stomp on the porch. Bang on the door.
> Make me get out of bed and come
> And let you in and light a light.

The speaker's demands are strong and insistent: *Come, Come, Come, Stomp, Bang, Make me*. The qualities of the speaker are unmistakable: he or she is enthusiastic, action oriented, and optimistic. The next lines go on to describe more about the speaker in only a few words:

> Tell me the northern lights are on
> And make me look. Or tell me clouds
> Are doing something to the moon
> They never did before, and show me.
> See that I see. . . .

The speaker's confidence and enthusiasm that clouds can be caught doing something they never did before is intriguing. You, the reader, are picked up and carried along by the speaker's feelings. By the end of the poem, you may have the feeling that by not being fully awake in life you have missed out on exciting and impressive experiences. You may begin to wonder with the speaker why you "ever went to bed at all."

The things that make this poem so effective are the language and the intensity that the speaker uses to describe his or her experiences. The speaker introduces you to an important idea and inspires you to make more of an effort to appreciate life in the same ways that he or she does.

EXERCISE 1

Reread the poems in Group 1. Then use what you have learned in this lesson to answer the following questions:

1. How does the speaker in "An Announcement" feel toward the person he or she is addressing? What details suggest the speaker's feelings? What will make it impossible for the other person to satisfy the speaker's demands?

2. Compare and contrast the poems "Look at Me" and "Summons." How are the speakers' tones alike or different? How are the poems' themes alike or different? Have you ever felt like either of these speakers? Why or why not?

Now check your answers with your teacher. Review this part of the lesson if you don't understand why an answer was incorrect.

WRITING ON YOUR OWN 1

You have learned that poetry can be an intensely personal communication between a poet and a reader. In this exercise you will focus on issues that you feel are important enough to write a poem about. Follow these steps:

- Get together with a small group of classmates. You will work with this group to complete the rest of the writing exercises in this unit.
- Along the left side of a sheet of paper, have one member of the group (called the recorder) list these school-related topics: music class, gym class, lunch time, friends, the school bus, celebration of holidays at school, school assemblies.

• Next to each topic, have the recorder list different members' feelings about it. For example, some group members may dislike the noise and the rough ride on the school bus, but other members may find the ride fun because they can talk to their friends there. Record the feelings of all group members.

LESSON 2   A POEM USES FORMS AND SOUND

The form of most poems is different from that of prose. Poems are written in lines that are clustered together in groups called *stanzas*. Unlike prose sentences, which run one after another in paragraphs, the break between two lines of poetry may come in the middle of a sentence. A poem may not even use capital letters to begin sentences or punctuation to end them. Readers must give full attention to the appearance of a poem in order to decide where there are logical breaks between ideas.

In many poems there are logical breaks between stanzas. Poets use the stanza much as they do a paragraph, with all of the lines of the stanza related. Sometimes a line, a pair of lines, or a whole stanza is repeated. These repeated lines or stanzas are called *refrains*.

When you look at the three poems in Group 2, you will find that only one of them, "Western Wagons," is divided into stanzas. A careful reading of the poem, stanza by stanza, will show a definite arrangement of ideas. In stanza 1 a narrator—called a *speaker*—sets the scene and brings in the pioneers to speak for themselves. In stanza 2 the characters describe their present actions and short-term goals. Stanza 3 once more begins with the voice of the speaker and switches to the pioneers. In the final stanza the pioneers make predictions about the future.

In addition to this development of ideas, there is an obvious arrangement in the form of "Western Wagons." This poem is one of many that use patterns in sound. One of these patterns uses *rhythm*, the regular appearance of stressed syllables in the flow of the language. Another pattern uses *rhyme*, the repetition of certain sounds in words.

In "Western Wagons" the rhythmic pattern is easy to hear. In fact, the phrase "Susanna, don't you cry!" reminds us of a familiar song and suggests how singable the poem is. The pattern of rhyme is also unmistakable. Notice how there is a natural pause at the end of every line so that we can easily hear and compare the rhyming pairs *are/far* and *Ioway/today* at the ends of these lines:

> We've broken land and cleared it, but we're tired of
>   where we are.
> They say that wild Nebraska is a better place by far.
> There's gold in far Wyoming, there's black earth in
>   Ioway,
> So pack up the kids and blankets, for we're moving
> out today!

The poets even use a nonstandard spelling of *Iowa* to make sure that readers pronounce the name in a way that will rhyme with *today*.

In contrast to "Western Wagons," the poem "Legacies" does not use stanzas, capitalization, or end punctuation. It also has no single rhythm—that is, it has no regular pattern of stressed syllables. However, the poem is written in lines, and the appearance of the lines gives a clue to the organization of thoughts. The unexpected breaks between lines, as in the following passage, force the reader to slow down and think about what is happening:

> "i want chu to learn how to make rolls" said the
> old woman proudly

but the little girl didn't want
to learn how because she knew
even if she couldn't say it that
that would mean when the old one died she would be
   less
dependent on her spirit so
she said
   "i don't want to know how to make no rolls"

In listening to this poem, even if you miss the impact of the line breaks, you will hear the contrasting voices of the speaker, the old woman, and the little girl.

As you can see by these two examples, poetry comes in a wide variety of forms. "Western Wagons" puts more emphasis on the patterns of sound, whereas "Legacies" stresses the appearance of the lines. To appreciate a poem fully, you need to be aware of the poem's form and think about why the poet chose it. Then you must adapt your reading style to the style of the poem to unlock all that it has to say.

EXERCISE 2

Reread the poems in Group 2. Then use what you have learned in this lesson to answer the following questions.

1. Both "Western Wagons" and "Legacies" feature speakers who set the scene and comment on it, as well as characters who speak directly to us. However, the poems use different methods to set off visually the words of the characters from the words of the speakers. Explain both of the methods.

2. What is unique about the appearance of the words in "Pure Poetry"? How does the appearance of the poem contribute to its meaning?

Now check your answers with your teacher. Review this part of the lesson if you don't understand why an answer was incorrect.

WRITING ON YOUR OWN [2]

You have seen how some poets use rhyme and rhythm to communicate their messages. Now you and your group will have a chance to write some rhymes and rhythms of your own. Follow these steps:

- For each of the following words, think of as many rhyming words as you can. Have one member of the group record everyone's suggestions.

  school　room　hall　feature

- Now, using rhyming words from your lists, write a two-line poem for each of the four original words. If you can, try to write poems that have regular rhythm.

LESSON 3 | A POEM PAINTS A PICTURE WITH WORDS

Usually when people are asked to write a poem, they set to work trying to think of rhyming words that they can match up with a catchy rhythm. Although it is true that poems often do rhyme and that some have a definite rhythm, many other poems do not. The next time someone asks you to write a poem, instead of trying to make a rhyme, consider painting a picture with words—whether they rhyme or not.

Another name for a word picture is an *image*. Poets often try to recreate experiences they have had, and the only tools they can work with are words. Often poets appeal to your senses by using small, easily pictured details to create a particular image. For example, in "Write About a Radish," Karla Kuskin uses details to make you feel the beauty and stillness of a dark night. To which of your senses does she appeal in these lines from the poem?

> The night is black
> The stars are small and high
> The clock unwinds its ever-ticking tune
> Hills gleam dimly
> Distant nighthawks cry.

As you read this poem you begin to see the black sky with its tiny, faraway stars, and you can see hills in the distance. You hear the clock "ever-ticking" and the lonely sound of the nighthawks crying. The poet's words appeal to both your sense of sight and your sense of hearing.

This peaceful picture is interrupted by the last line of the poem, however: "A radish rises in the waiting sky." A radish? At first you are being lulled into a calm mood, reflecting on the beauty of the night, and suddenly your mind is forced to see an unexpected image that breaks the quietness and makes you laugh. The image of the rising radish also makes the poet's point—try to see the world in a new way, to shake things up a little.

Sometimes the best way to see reality is by drawing comparisons between things that usually are not connected. When you analyze what makes these things alike, you are able to see each thing more clearly. In "Your World" poet Georgia Douglas Johnson compares herself to a bird:

> Your world is as big as you make it.
> I know, for I used to abide
> In the narrowest nest in a corner,
> My wings pressing close to my side.

The speaker believes that he or she is like a young bird, too timid to risk leaving the safety of the nest. However, at some point a change occurs within the speaker.

I battered the cordons around me
And cradled my wings on the breeze
Then soared to the uttermost reaches
With rapture, with power, with ease!

The speaker is now like a bird that has found its wings.
It feels the freedom that can come only when one decides
to abandon security and take a chance. The comparison
between the speaker and the bird allows readers to understand the profound change that has taken place within the
person.

EXERCISE 3

Reread "Your Poem, Man . . ." and then use what you have
learned in this lesson to answer the following questions.

1. Which two images in the poem do you like best? What do
   you like about each of them—the visual picture it paints,
   the surprise it gave you when you first read it, or something else?

2. The speaker is encouraging poets to try to make unusual
   connections to describe and share their feelings about the
   world. Do you agree that telling "it like it never really was"
   helps us "see it like it is"? Why or why not?

Now check your answers with your teacher. Review this
part of the lesson if you don't understand why an answer
was incorrect.

 ## WRITING ON YOUR OWN 3

In this exercise you will make a list of details to describe a
location in your school. Follow these steps:

- Together with your group think of various places that you all know well. These places should relate to school in some way. For example, you might all walk down a certain hall or meet for class in a certain room or eat in the same lunchroom. Look over your list and choose one place that you all can picture most clearly.
- Now brainstorm a list of details about the place. Your details can describe things you see, hear, smell, taste, or touch in that location. They also can describe the way you feel when you are there. If possible, include one unusual comparison in your list of details.
- When you are finished with your list, share it with the other groups in your class.

DISCUSSION GUIDES

1. What were your feelings about poetry before you began
   this unit? Had you enjoyed it in the past, or did you find it
   confusing? Were there only a few poems that appealed to
   you, or did you find many worth reading or memorizing?
   What elements of poetry mentioned in this unit's overview
   sound most interesting to you? After discussing these
   questions with your class, work together to draw up a
   questionnaire of three to five questions about people's attitudes toward poetry. Make sure your questions can be
   answered with the word *yes* or *no* or with a number from 1
   to 10. Have everyone in the class answer the questionnaire, and then score the results. Save the questionnaire
   until you finish this book. Then ask the questions a second
   time to see whether anyone's attitude toward poetry—or
   appreciation of it—has changed.

2. In some of the poems in Unit 1, only one speaker appears.
   In others, two, three, or more speakers have their say.
   Choose a poem that you would like to present to an audience. If the poem has more than one speaker, ask some
   classmates to join you in the presentation. Decide who
   should read which lines. If the poem has only one speaker,
   practice your presentation by yourself. Let your teacher
   know when you and any classmates are ready to present
   the poem to your class.

3. Of all the poems in this unit, which ones would you like to
   have written yourself? Choose no more than three. Why
   did you make those choices? Would you expect everyone
   else to make the same choices? Why or why not?
   Compare your choices and your reasons for choosing
   them with others' choices and reasons.

WRITE A GROUP POEM

In this unit you have been introduced to what poetry is and how it is different from prose. In the writing exercises you have started to think like a poet. Now you will work with a group to write an original poem about school.

Follow these steps to write your poem. If you have questions about the writing process, refer to Using the Writing Process (page 235).

- Review the work you did for all the writing exercises in this unit: 1) a list of details about things in your life that you feel strongly about, 2) descriptions of your feelings about school-related topics, 3) four two-line rhyming poems, 4) a list of details about a particular location.
- Decide on a particular school-related place for your group poem. Make sure you have plenty of descriptive details to choose from.
- Decide on the feeling you would like to communicate through your poem. For example, do you want your poem to be funny, exciting, or suspenseful? Discuss how you all feel about the place and which mood you want to convey about it.
- Decide whether your poem will rhyme. Although some people find it easier to write a poem that doesn't rhyme, you may decide that rhyme will add to the mood or make your poem more effective.
- Now write your group poem. Make it between 6 and 24 lines long. Refer to the previous writing exercises for details to include. Also include at least one unusual comparison.
- Have one member of your group reread the poem aloud. Does it communicate the feeling you had planned? Why or why not? Does the comparison work? Do the poem's details paint a clear image? Make any changes or additions that will help improve the poem.
- Proofread the poem for any spelling, grammar, punctuation, capitalization, and formatting errors. Then have one or more group members read it aloud to the class.

Voices in Poetry

The Windmill
by Henry Wadsworth Longfellow

The Builders
by Sara Henderson Hay

To Satch
by Samuel Allen

Oranges
by Gary Soto

Oranges
by Jean Little

Argument
by Eve Merriam

There Is No Word for Goodbye
by Mary TallMountain

The Glove and the Lions
by Leigh Hunt

Dorlan's Home-Walk
by Arthur Guiterman

The Stone
by Wilfrid Wilson Gibson

INTRODUCTION

**ABOUT THE
LESSONS**

In every poem, you hear a voice speaking to you. Sometimes it is the voice of the poet himself or herself. At other times, however, you hear another character speaking to you. The poet may write using the voice of a person he or she knows or imagines or the voice of a snake in the grass, a bird in the sky, or even a wooden fence. In a way, the poet becomes that person, animal, or object and imagines what he, she, or it would say.

In this unit you will hear the voices of speakers in eleven poems. The poems are divided into three groups. In the first group you will read poems in which the speaker is someone or something other than the poet. The second group includes poems in which you overhear the speaker talking to himself or herself and poems in which you hear two voices. In the third group you will read stories told by a narrator speaking from the first-person or the third-person point of view.

 WRITING: DEVELOPING SPEAKERS

In this unit you will write a short poem using the imagined voice of a speaker who is an animal or an object. Begin thinking about the speaker you will develop. Here are some suggestions:

- Make a list of animals whose habits you know well, such as your pet cat or dog. You may wish to include wild animals, such as squirrels or birds, in your list. Observe the animals for a while and make notes on their actions.
- Make another list, this time of objects that you use every day. Try to imagine what it would feel like to be each of those objects and make some notes about your thoughts.
- Save your list to refer to in later writing exercises.

ABOUT THIS POET

Gary Soto (1952–) was born and raised in Fresno, California. During the Depression his grandparents had moved there from Mexico to find work as farm laborers. Soto graduated from California State University at Fresno and later earned the degree of Master of Fine Arts in Creative Writing at University of California at Irvine.

Although he may be best known for his poetry, he has also written essays, short stories, and novels for both young readers and adults. His first published book of poetry, *The Elements of San Joaquin*, was given the United States Award of the International Poetry Forum. In 1985 his book of autobiographical essays, *Living up the Street*, won the Before Columbus Foundation American Book Award. The American Library Association named his short story collection *Baseball in April* as one of its Best Books for Young Adults. His video *Pool Party* won the Andrew Carnegie Medal for Excellence in Children's video in 1993, and in 1995 Soto was nominated for a National Book Award.

The poet often writes about the lives of Mexican Americans, drawing on his experiences growing up in Fresno. His poems are usually simple and direct, using clear images and exact words.

Soto now lives with his wife and daughter in Berkeley, California, where he is a professor at the University of California.

AS YOU READ

As you read the poems in this unit, keep these questions in mind:

- Who is the speaker in each poem?
- What do you learn about the personality of the speaker by what he or she says?
- Why does the poet choose that particular speaker for the poem?

The Windmill

by Henry Wadsworth Longfellow

ABOUT THE SELECTION

Henry Wadsworth Longfellow (1807–1882) was one of the most popular American poets of the 19th century. Born in Portland, Maine, Longfellow attended Bowdoin College along with fellow writer Nathaniel Hawthorne. After graduating, he became a professor of modern languages, first at Bowdoin and then at Harvard College. Longfellow taught at Harvard for 18 years before retiring to devote all his energies to his writing career. Some of his more famous poems include "The Village Blacksmith" and "The Wreck of the Hesperus." He is also remembered for his long narrative poems, including "Evangeline" and "The Song of Hiawatha." In the following poem, "The Windmill," he assumes the identity of a structure that once was a familiar sight on the New England landscape.

Behold! a giant am I!
   Aloft here in my tower,
   With my granite jaws I devour
The maize, and the wheat, and the rye,
   And grind them into flour.

I look down over the farms;
   In the fields of grain I see
   The harvest that is to be,
And I fling to the air my arms,
   For I know it is all for me.

I hear the sounds of flails[1]
    Far off, from the threshing-floors[2]
    In barns, with their open doors,
And the wind, the wind in my sails,
    Louder and louder roars.

I stand here in my place,
    With my foot on the rock below,
    And whichever way it may blow,
I meet it face to face
    As a brave man meets his foe.

And while we wrestle and strive,
    My master, the miller, stands
    and feeds me with his hands;
For he knows who makes him thrive,[3]
    Who makes him lord of lands.

On Sundays I take my rest;
    Church-going bells begin
    Their low, melodious din;
I cross my arms on my breast,
    And all is peace within.

---

[1] a farm tool with free-swinging sticks at the end of a long handle, used to beat grain from its husk

[2] areas where grain is beaten from its husk

[3] to be successful; to prosper

The Builders

by Sara Henderson Hay

ABOUT THE SELECTION

Sara Henderson Hay (1906–1987) was born in Pittsburgh, Pennsylvania. She attended Breneau College and Columbia University. This poem is taken from her book *Story Hour* in which she takes an unusual look at traditional tales and legends.

I told them a thousand times if I told them once:
Stop fooling around, I said, with straw and sticks;
They won't hold up; you're taking an awful chance.
Brick is the stuff to build with, solid bricks.
You want to be impractical, go ahead.
But just remember, I told them; wait and see.
You're making a big mistake. Awright, I said,
But when the wolf comes, don't come running to me.

The funny thing is, they didn't. There they sat,
One in his crummy yellow shack, and one
Under his roof of twigs, and the wolf ate
Them, hair and hide. Well, what is done is done.
But I'd been willing to help them, all along,
If only they'd once admitted they were wrong.

To Satch

by Samuel Allen

ABOUT THE SELECTION

Poet Samuel Allen (1917–   ) studied law at Harvard University and the Sorbonne in Paris, but decided to become a poet and a teacher of African-American literature instead of a lawyer. In this poem he writes about Leroy "Satchel" Paige who was a great pitcher in the Negro League and is now a member of the Baseball Hall of Fame.

Sometimes I feel like I will never stop
Just go on forever
Till one fine mornin'
I'm gonna reach up and grab me
    a handfulla stars
Throw out my long lean leg
And whip three hot strikes burnin'
    down the heavens
And look over at God and say
How about that!

Oranges

by Gary Soto

ABOUT THE SELECTION

Gary Soto (1952–   ) has won awards for both his poetry and his prose. Born in Fresno, California, he often focuses on the lives and experiences of Mexican Americans. For more information about Gary Soto, see About This Poet at the beginning of this unit. Look for the realistic details about daily life in the following poem, "Oranges."

The first time I walked
With a girl, I was twelve.
Cold, and weighted down
With two oranges in my jacket.
December. Frost crackling
Beneath my steps, my breath
Before me, then gone,
As I walked toward
Her house, the one whose
Porchlight burned yellow
Night and day, in any weather.
A dog barked at me, until
She came out pulling
At her gloves, face bright
With rouge. I smiled,
Touched her shoulder, and led
Her down the street, across
A used car lot and a line
Of newly planted trees,
Until we were breathing

Before a drug store. We
Entered, the tiny bell
Bringing a saleslady
Down a narrow aisle of goods.
I turned to the candies
Tiered like bleachers,
And asked what she wanted—
Light in her eyes, a smile
Starting at the corners
Of her mouth. I fingered
A nickel in my pocket,
And when she lifted a chocolate
That cost a dime,
I didn't say anything.
I took the nickel from
My pocket, then an orange,
And set them quietly on
The counter. When I looked up,
The lady's eyes met mine,
And held them, knowing
Very well what it was all
About.

     Outside,
A few cars hissing past,
Fog hanging like old
Coats between the trees.
I took my girl's hand
In mine for two blocks,
Then released it to let
Her unwrap the chocolate.
I peeled my orange
That was so bright against
The gray of December
That, from some distance,
Someone might have thought
I was making a fire in my hands.

Oranges

by Jean Little

ABOUT THE SELECTION

Jean Little (1932–) has written both short stories and poems for young readers. Almost blind, she often highlights the special needs of the disabled and the importance of friendship. Which of those themes do you see in this poem?

I peel oranges neatly.
The sections come apart cleanly, perfectly, in my hands.

When Emily peels an orange, she tears holes in it.
Juice squirts in all directions.

"Kate," she says, "I don't know how you do it!"

Emily is my best friend.
I hope she never learns how to peel oranges.

Argument

by Eve Merriam

ABOUT THE SELECTION

Eve Merriam (1916–1992) received a number of awards for her poetry, plays, and fiction. She wrote more than 30 books, many of them for young readers. Her poetry often focuses on social issues, such as women's rights. "Argument" is like a mini-play to be acted out using two voices.

Good morning.
     Hmmm.
Nice day.
     Dim.
Sorry.
     Glad.
Hadn't.
     Had.
Go.
     Stay.
     Work.
Play.

Pro.
     Con.
Off.
     On.
Front.
     Back.
     Taut.
Slack.
Open.
     Shut.
And.
     But.

Over.
     Under.
Cloudless.
     Thunder.
Detour.
     Highway.
New way.
     Thruway.
Byway . . . ?
     MY WAY!

There Is No Word for Goodbye

by Mary TallMountain

ABOUT THE SELECTION

Mary TallMountain (1918–   ) was born in Nulato, Alaska, into the Koykon-Athabaskan people. When Mary was quite young, her mother became ill, and Mary was adopted by a white family. After some difficult times she became an advocate for the homeless. Today she lives in San Francisco, California. In many of her poems, including the one you are about to read, she recalls her Athabaskan heritage.

Sokoya, I said, looking through
    the net of wrinkles into
    wise black pools
    of her eyes.

What do you say in Athabaskan
    when you leave each other?
    What is the word
    for goodbye?

A shade of feeling rippled
    the wind-tanned skin.
    Ah, nothing, she said,
    watching the river flash.

She looked at me close.
        We just say, Tlaa. That means,
        See you.
        We never leave each other.
        When does your mouth
        say goodbye to your heart?

She touched me light
        as a bluebell.
        You forget when you leave us,
        You're so small then.
        We don't use that word.

We always think you're coming back
        but if you don't,
        we'll see you some place else.
        You understand,
                There is no word for goodbye.

The Glove and the Lions

by Leigh Hunt

ABOUT THE SELECTION

Leigh Hunt (1784–1859) was a friend of many of the great English poets of his time. In addition to writing poetry, he was the editor of a magazine. At one point, his radical political opinions landed him in jail for a three-year period, but he continued to write in spite of his imprisonment.

King Francis was a hearty king, and loved a royal sport,
And one day, as his lions fought, sat looking on the court.
The nobles filled the benches, and the ladies in their pride,
And 'mongst them sat the Count de Lorge, with one for
    whom he sighed:
And truly 'twas a gallant thing to see the crowning show,
Valor and love, and a king above, and the royal beasts below.

Ramped[1] and roared the lions, with horrid laughing jaws;
They bit, they glared, gave blows like beams, a wind went
    with their paws;
With wallowing might and stifled roar they rolled on one
    another,
Till all the pit with sand and mane was in a thunderous
    smother;

---

[1] stood with forelegs raised

46

The bloody foam above the bars came whisking through
   the air;
Said Francis then, "Faith, gentlemen, we're better here
   than there."
De Lorge's love o'erheard the King, a beauteous lively
   dame,
With smiling lips and sharp bright eyes, which always
   seemed the same;
She thought, "The Count, my lover, is brave as brave can
   be;
He surely would do wondrous things to show his love of
   me;
King, ladies, lovers, all look on; the occasion is divine;
I'll drop my glove to prove his love; great glory will be
   mine."

She dropped her glove, to prove his love, then looked at
   him and smiled;
He bowed, and in a moment leaped among the lions wild;
The leap was quick, return was quick, he had regained his
   place,
Then threw the glove, but not with love, right in the lady's
   face.
"By Heaven," said Francis, "rightly done!" and he rose from
   where he sat;
"No love," quoth he, "but vanity,[2] sets love a task like
   that."

---

[2] pride and conceit

Dorlan's Home-Walk

by Arthur Guiterman

ABOUT THE SELECTION

Arthur Guiterman (1871–1943) was a poet and journalist who specialized in writing poetry about incidents from America's past. His poems appeared in popular magazines such as *Life* and the *Saturday Evening Post*. In his thousands of published poems, he shows a sense of humor and an appreciation for traditional rhymes and rhythms. In "Dorlan's Home-Walk" he takes a light look at one of America's favorite pastimes— baseball.

The ninth; last half; the score was tied,
    The hour was big with fate,
For Neal had fanned and Kling had flied
    When Dorlan toed the plate.

And every rooter drew a breath
    And rose from where he sat,
For weal or woe,[1] or life or death
    Now hung on Dorlan's bat.

The pitcher scowled; the pitcher flung
    An inshoot, swift and queer;
But Dorlan whirled his wagon-tongue
    And smote the leathern sphere.

---

[1] good or bad

He smote the ball with might and main,
    He drove it long and low,
And firstward like a railway train
    He sped to beat the throw.

He reached first base with time to spare
    (The throw went high and wide),
But what a tumult[2] rent[3] the air
    When "Safe!" the umpire cried.

"What!" shrieked the pitcher, lean
      and tall,
    "What!" roared the catcher stout,
"Wha-at!" yelled the basemen one
      and all,
    "Ye're off! the man is out!"

The shortstop swore, the catcher pled,
    They waved their arms around.
The umpire shook his bullet-head
    And sternly held his ground,

Though in the wild-eyed fielders ran
    To tear him limb from limb
Or else to tell that erring man
    Just what they thought of *him*.

The basemen left the bases clear
    And came to urge their case—
So Dorlan yawned and scratched his ear
    And strolled to second base.

---

[2] confusion and uproar

[3] split or tore apart

"Safe? Safe?" the pitcher hissed. "Ye're
     blind!"
  And breathed a naughty word;
While Dorlan hitched his belt behind
  And rambled on to third.

And throats were hoarse and words ran
     high
  And lips were flecked with foam,
As Dorlan scanned the azure sky
  And ambled on toward home.

And still he heard in dreamy bliss,
  As down the line he came,
The umpire growl, "Enough o' this!
  He's safe. Now play the game!"

"All right. Come, boys," the pitcher
     bawled,
  "Two out; now make it three!"
When Dorlan touched the plate and
     drawled,
  "Hey! score that run fer me!"

What wrath was there, what bitter talk,
  What joy and wild acclaim!
For Dorlan's peaceful homeward walk
  Had won the doubtful game.

Aye, thus the game was lost and won;
  So, athletes, great and small,
If like mischance ye fain would shun[4]
  Keep cool, don't kick, play ball.

---

[4] if you would like to avoid a similar misfortune

The Stone

by Wilfrid Wilson Gibson

ABOUT THE SELECTION

Wilfrid Wilson Gibson (1878–1962) was an English writer who published more than 22 volumes of poetry. Early in his career he wrote long poems about romantic historical characters, but his later work more often focused on difficult and painful issues such as war and poverty and the lives of common people. "The Stone" is the tragic story of a young woman grieving for her lost love.

"And will you cut a stone for him,
To set above his head?
And will you cut a stone for him—
A stone for him?" she said.

Three days before, a splintered rock
Had struck her lover dead—
Had struck him in the quarry dead,
Where careless of the warning call,
He loitered, while the shot was fired—
A lively stripling, brave and tall,
And sure of all his heart desired . . .
A flash, a shock,
A rumbling fall . . .
And, broken 'neath the broken rock,
A lifeless heap, with face of clay,
And still as any stone he lay,
With eyes that saw the end of all.

I went to break the news to her:
And I could hear my own heart beat
With dread of what my lips might say;
But some poor fool had sped before;
And, flinging wide her father's door,
Had blurted out the news to her,
Had struck her lover dead for her,
Had struck the girl's heart dead in her,
Had struck life, lifeless, at a word,
And dropped it at her feet:
Then hurried on his witless way,
Scarce knowing she had heard.
And when I came, she stood alone—
A woman, turned to stone:
And, though no word at all she said,
I knew that all was known.

Because her heart was dead,
She did not sigh nor moan.
His mother wept:
She could not weep.
Her lover slept:
She could not sleep.
Three days, three nights,
She did not stir:
Three days, three nights,
Were one to her,
Who never closed her eyes
From sunset to sunrise,
From dawn to evenfall—
Her tearless, staring eyes,
That, seeing naught,[1] saw all.

---

[1] nothing

The fourth night when I came from work,
I found her at my door.
"And will you cut a stone for him?"
She said: and spoke no more:
But followed me, as I went in,
And sank upon a chair;
And fixed her grey eyes on my face,
With still, unseeing stare.
And, as she waited patiently,
I could not bear to feel
Those still, grey eyes that followed me,
Those eyes that plucked the heart from me,
Those eyes that sucked the breath from me
And curdled the warm blood in me,
Those eyes that cut me to the bone,
And pierced my marrow[2] like cold steel.

And so I rose, and sought a stone;
And cut it, smooth and square:
And, as I worked, she sat and watched,
Beside me, in her chair.
Night after night, by candlelight,
I cut her lover's name:
Night after night, so still and white,
And like a ghost she came;
And sat beside me, in her chair,
And watched with eyes aflame.
She eyed each stroke,
And hardly stirred:
She never spoke
A single word:
And not a sound or murmur broke
The quiet, save the mallet-stroke.

---

[2] core; innermost or essential part

With still eyes ever on my hands,
With eyes that seemed to burn my hands,
My wincing, overwearied hands,
She watched, with bloodless lips apart,
And silent, indrawn breath:
And every stroke my chisel cut,
Death cut still deeper in her heart:
The two of us were chiselling,
Together, I and death.

And when at length the job was done,
And I had laid the mallet by,
As if, at last, her peace were won,
She breathed his name; and, with a sigh,
Passed slowly through the open door;
And never crossed my threshold more.

Next night I labored late, alone,
To cut her name upon the stone.

UNDERSTANDING THE POEMS

Record your answers to these questions in your personal literature notebook. Follow the directions for each group.

GROUP 1

Reread the poems in Group 1 to complete these sentences.

Reviewing the Selection

1. The speaker in "The Builders" insists that houses should be built of
  a. straw.
  b. sticks.
  c. logs.
  d. bricks.

2. What or whom does the speaker in "The Windmill" think of as its master?
  a. the miller
  b. the wind
  c. the threshers
  d. the grain it grinds

Interpreting the Selection

3. In "To Satch" when the speaker says "*How about that!*" it seems that he is
  a. feeling stronger than God.
  b. asking God for more physical ability.
  c. feeling proud of his abilities and is showing them off.
  d. asking if God approves of how he has rearranged the stars.

Recognizing How Words Are Used

4. What vowel sound is repeated in the following line from "The Windmill": "Their low, melodious din"?
  a. long *a*
  b. long *o*
  c. short *i*
  d. short *u*

Appreciating Poetry

5. The attitude, or tone, of the speaker in "The Builders" can best be described as
a. sympathetic and kind.
b. mysterious.
c. practical and slightly impatient.
d. joyful.

GROUP 2

Reread the poems in Group 2 to complete these sentences.

Reviewing the Selection

6. The speaker in Gary Soto's "Oranges" doesn't tell the girl that he can't afford the candy that costs a dime because he
a. is sure that the saleslady will accept an orange and a nickel instead.
b. is too embarrassed to admit that he doesn't have enough money.
c. thinks that the price is too high and wants to barter.
d. wants to get rid of one of the oranges anyway.

7. In "There Is No Word for Goodbye," Sokoya says that there is no word for *goodbye* in Athabaskan because
a. she knows that Athabaskans never really leave each other.
b. she is embarrassed because she has forgotten the word.
c. she doesn't want the speaker to leave.
d. the Athabaskan language is not developed enough.

Interpreting the Selection

8. One theme, or message, of Jean Little's "Oranges" might be that
a. the best way to keep a friend is to share with him or her.
b. if you want to keep a friend, you must have unusual abilities.
c. everyone likes to feel special at times.
d. some people focus too much on unimportant things.

Recognizing How Words Are Used

9. A *simile* compares one thing to another thing that is like it in some way. An example of a simile is
   a. Fog hanging like old/Coats between the trees.
   b. Open/Shut.
   c. The sections come apart cleanly, perfectly, in my hands.
   d. She looked at me close./We just say, Tlaa. That means/See you.

Appreciating Poetry

10. You learn all of the following in "Argument" *except* that
   a. both speakers are to blame for the argument.
   b. both speakers are angry and unreasonable.
   c. no matter what one speaker says, the other will say the opposite.
   d. the second speaker is smarter than the first.

GROUP 3

Reread the poems in Group 3 to complete these sentences.

Reviewing the Selection

11. In "The Glove and the Lions" the beautiful lady drops her glove among the lions because
   a. she is careless and clumsy.
   b. she wants to see the lions chew it up.
   c. that is one of the rules of the sport.
   d. she wants her lover to prove his love for her.

12. After he retrieves the glove, her lover throws it in her face because
   a. he doesn't want a lover who puts him in danger for her own amusement.
   b. he has bad aim and meant to toss it lightly into her lap.
   c. King Francis ordered him to do so.
   d. that is the way dropped gloves are traditionally returned.

Interpreting the
Selection

13. In "The Stone" the speaker says that a fool who told the girl that her lover was dead had struck the girl's heart dead and dropped it at her feet. What the speaker means here is that the fool had
   a. hit the girl and made her fall to the floor.
   b. made the girl lose her ability to feel by the way he told her the news.
   c. cut out the girl's heart and dropped it at her feet.
   d. caused the girl's heart to stop beating.

Appreciating Poetry

14. The mood of "The Stone" can be described as
   a. shocking.
   b. lighthearted.
   c. hopeful.
   d. sorrowful.

Recognizing How
Words Are Used

15. The speaker in "Dorlan's Home-Walk" uses words that are more elegant than those used by most people. When the speaker says that "Dorlan whirled his wagon-tongue," he or she means that Dorlan
   a. taunted the pitcher.
   b. swung the bat.
   c. curled his tongue.
   d. argued with the umpire.

Now check your answers with your teacher. Study the questions you answered incorrectly. What types of questions were they? Talk with your teacher about ways to work on those skills.

Voices in Poetry

The telephone rings and you answer it. Sometimes you immediately recognize the speaker's voice as that of a friend or relative. At other times, however, the voice is not familiar. To identify it, you need to listen to what the speaker is saying and how he or she is saying it. For example, the voice may be that of a neighbor in trouble. He or she may be speaking so excitedly that the message is hard to follow. After you identify the neighbor's voice, however, you probably will begin to understand what the conversation is about.

In the same way, you find a poem and begin to read it. Sometimes the speaker's voice is easy to identify. Often it is the voice of the poet speaking to you. At other times, however, you might feel confused. Who is speaking? Again, in order to understand the message of the poem, you need to pay attention to the clues that the speaker gives.

In the following lessons you will learn how to recognize the ways in which poets create and reveal the speakers in their poems:

1. Instead of using their own voice and point of view, poets may use the voice and point of view of a different person or character, an animal, or an object.

2. The poet may use monologues and dialogues to represent various speakers.

3. The poet may create a speaker who narrates a story from the first-person or third-person point of view.

LESSON 1 | IDENTIFYING THE SPEAKER OR SPEAKERS IN A POEM

When you wake up each morning, you know exactly who you are. You are a certain age and sex, you live at a particular address, and you go to the same school that you went to yesterday. You are defined and limited by your reality. If you were the speaker in a poem, however, you could break free from reality's limitations. You could be a fish swimming through a dark cave or a race-car driver rounding a turn. You could take on the personality of a new character and write as if you were him, her, or it. To speak as a new character, all you need is a good imagination.

In "The Windmill" poet Henry Wadsworth Longfellow speaks as a windmill. In order to speak from the windmill's point of view, the poet imagines a new voice, called a *persona*, a word that comes from the Latin word meaning "mask." The persona is not the poet but is instead a new character. Notice that the poem begins boldly, as if a human speaker filled with energy and strength were talking. However, an important clue in the third line alerts you that the speaker cannot be human:

> Behold! a giant am I!
>   Aloft here in my tower,
>   With my granite jaws I devour
> The maize, and the wheat, and the rye,
>   And grind them into flour.

Since no human could have "granite jaws," you conclude that the speaker must be the windmill itself. Not only does Longfellow speak as an object throughout the poem; he also gives the windmill a personality. The windmill sees its mission as indispensable to the miller, and it is proud of its own daring against the power of the wind.

You probably assumed, at first, that the speaker of "The Builders" was a human. The first few lines made you aware that the person speaking is self-satisfied and bossy, but there was no hint that he or she was not human. However, as you continued to read, clues in the poem probably made you wonder about the speaker's identity.

Stop fooling around, I said, with straw and sticks;
They won't hold up; you're taking an awful chance.
Brick is the stuff to build with, solid bricks.

Straw, sticks, bricks—you have heard about these mate-
rials somewhere before. A few lines later, when you read
about the wolf, you probably knew for sure that the speaker
is the last remaining little pig from the familiar folktale
"The Three Little Pigs." Now you know what the practical
little pig thinks as he sits in his sturdy brick house all alone.
He is proud of his intelligence, but he also is confused and
disappointed that the other two pigs didn't listen to him.

EXERCISE 1

Reread "To Satch" and then use what you learned in this
lesson to answer the following questions:

1. Who is the speaker in this poem? At what point did you
   recognize the speaker's identity?

2. How would you describe the speaker's personality—proud,
   fun-loving, arrogant, strong, or some combination of these
   qualities? Do you think that you would like to have the
   speaker as a friend? Why or why not?

3. How do you think the poet feels about Satch? Explain the
   reasons for your answer.

Now check your answers with your teacher. Review this
part of the lesson if you don't understand why an answer
was incorrect.

WRITING ON YOUR OWN 1

At the beginning of this unit you started listing possible
animals or objects that could be the speakers in your

poems. Now you will choose two of those animals or objects to be the possible speakers in your first poem. Follow these steps:

- Before you choose your speaker or speakers, decide whether your poem will be a monologue or a dialogue.
- Review your lists of animals and objects. At this point you may want to add other animals or objects if you find them more interesting.
- Look over your completed lists carefully. Then choose the two animals or objects that you can picture most clearly and make them the speakers of your poem.
- Think about what it would be like to be your chosen speakers. Then complete each of these sentence frames in at least three ways for each speaker:
  Being a(n) _____ would be enjoyable because _____.

  Being a(n) _____ would be difficult because _____.

LESSON 2 MONOLOGUE AND DIALOGUE IN POEMS

In many poems, you "overhear" the speaker talking to himself, herself, or itself. The speaker may be remembering a past experience or reflecting on an insight about life. Such poems are considered to be *monologues* because they are speeches made by one person. (Remember, *mono* means "one.")

Gary Soto's poem "Oranges" is an example of a monologue. In this poem, the speaker recalls "the first time I walked with a girl." The monologue reveals what happened that day, but it also reveals much about the speaker himself. For example, what do you learn about the speaker from these lines from the poem?

December. Frost cracking
Beneath my steps, my breath
Before me, then gone,
As I walked toward
Her house, the one whose
Porchlight burned yellow
Night and day, in any weather.
A dog barked at me, until
She came out pulling
At her gloves, face bright
With rouge.

Even years later as an adult, the speaker remembers
specific sensory details about the coldness of the day, the
sound of the frost cracking beneath his feet, the yellow
porchlight, and the brightness of the girl's rouge. The
speaker is clearly someone who is sensitive to the world
around him.

Oranges bring different thoughts to poet Jean Little's
mind. The speaker in her poem is not remembering something that happened years ago. Instead, the speaker's monologue involves a current friendship. She even repeats her
friend's exact words that mean so much to her. What do
you learn about the speaker from her words? Could the
speaker be the poet herself?

"Kate," she says, "I don't know how you do it!"

Emily is my best friend.
I hope she never learns how to peel oranges.

The speaker probably is not the poet herself. The
speaker's name is Kate, not Jean, and she is most likely a
young girl. Like most girls, she has a best friend with whom
she wants to feel special. By using a young person as the
speaker, the poet creates a poem that is simple, direct, and

real. When you read the poem, you share in the warm feelings that friendship brings.

Eve Merriam's "Argument" is an example of a poem in which more than one speaker engages in a conversation called a *dialogue*. In the following excerpt, how does the poet show you that two people are speaking?

> Good morning.
> > Hmmm.
> Nice day.
> > Dim.
> Sorry.
> > Glad.
> Hadn't.
> > Had.

The first speaker's words are printed in the left side of each column, and the second speaker's words appear in the right side of each column. The changing placement of the words emphasizes the fact that someone new is talking, as well as the back-and-forth, tug-of-war nature of most arguments.

EXERCISE [2]

Reread "There Is No Word for Goodbye." Then use what you have learned in this lesson to answer the following questions:

1. Which words in this poem are said by the speaker who is recalling the conversation? Which words are said by the woman whom the speaker calls Sokoya?

2. How would you describe Sokoya's age and personality? What clues help you paint a mental picture of the woman?

3. What do you know about the speaker from what he or she says and from what Sokoya says?

Now check your answers with your teacher. Review this part of the lesson if you don't understand why an answer was incorrect.

WRITING ON YOUR OWN 2

In Writing on Your Own 1, you chose two animals or objects to be the speakers of your first poem. Now you will write that poem. Follow these steps:

- If you plan to write a monologue, decide what your speaker will talk about. If your speaker were a telephone, for example, it might talk about the conversations it hears, how often it is used, or the people who use it. If the speaker were your family pet, it might talk about what it likes and dislikes about living with your family or in your home.
- If you plan to write a dialogue, imagine that your two chosen speakers are having a conversation. What might they be talking about? If your speakers were two dining-room chairs, for example, they might be talking about the difficulties they face during dinner parties. If your speakers were two animals in a zoo, they might be talking about all the fun they have while watching their visitors. If your speakers were a bird and a tree, they might be talking about how much they enjoy each other's company.
- Once you've decided what your monologue speaker or dialogue speakers will say, write a poem about the conversation.

LESSON 3 | NARRATIVE POEMS

Each poem in Group 3 is a *narrative poem*—a rather long poem that tells a story. Like all good stories, narrative poems have interesting characters who are faced with conflicts.

These conflicts build up to a *climax*, or moment of highest tension, and then wind down during the *falling action.*

All narrative poems are told by a *narrator.* Sometimes the narrator is outside the story and knows everything that is happening. This narrator tells the story from the *third-person* point of view, using the pronouns *he, she,* and *they.* At other times the narrator is part of the story and tells only what he or she sees happening. This narrator tells the story from the *first-person* point of view, using the pronouns *I* and *me.*

"The Glove and the Lions" is an example of a narrative poem told from the third-person point of view. Read the following lines from the poem to find evidence that the story is being told by an all-knowing narrator:

> De Lorge's love o'erheard the King, a beauteous lively dame,
> With smiling lips and sharp bright eyes, which always seemed the same;
> She thought, "The Count, my lover, is brave as brave can be:
> He surely would do wondrous things to show his love of me;

The narrator calls the woman *she* and can read her mind—a feat possible only by someone who can see and understand everything that is happening.

In contrast to the narrator in "The Glove and Lions," the narrator in "The Stone" is a participant in the action—the stonecutter. The stonecutter's point of view is limited only to what he or she can see and hear. This person cannot read the mind of the grieving woman but can help us feel what it is like to be around her and her sorrow:

> And, as she waited patiently,
> I could not bear to feel

Those still, grey eyes that followed me,
Those eyes that plucked the heart from me,
Those eyes that sucked the breath from me
And curdled the warm blood in me,
Those eyes that cut me to the bone,
And pierced my marrow like cold steel.

By making the narrator part of the sad situation, the poet pulls readers into the sorrow-filled world of the woman and the stonecutter.

EXERCISE 3

Reread the following excerpt from "Dorlan's Home-Walk." Then use what you have learned in this lesson to answer the questions that follow the excerpt.

What wrath was there, what bitter talk,
    What joy and wild acclaim!
For Dorlan's peaceful homeward walk
    Had won the doubtful game.

Aye, thus the game was lost and won;
    So, athletes, great and small,
If like mischance ye fain would shun
    Keep cool, don't kick, play ball.

1. Except for the last three lines, is the story in this narrative poem told from the first-person or the third-person point of view? How can you tell?

2. In the last three lines the narrator speaks directly to the reader and gives advice on how to play any game. What do you learn about the narrator from this advice? What is his or her attitude toward people who get upset about things instead of taking them in stride?

Now check your answers with your teacher. Review this part of the lesson if you don't understand why an answer was incorrect.

WRITING ON YOUR OWN 3

In this exercise you will use the first poem that you wrote to help you write a narrative poem. Follow these steps:

- Go back to your original list of animals and objects and choose one more speaker. Now imagine that this speaker overheard the conversation that you wrote about in your monologue or dialogue poem.
- Write a narrative poem in which your new speaker is the narrator. Decide whether your speaker will tell about the conversation from the first-person or third-person point of view. If you'd like, you can use parts of your first poem again in your narrative poem.

DISCUSSION GUIDES

1. Work with a few classmates to prepare oral readings of three or four of the poems in this unit. Choose the poems you like best and be sure that at least one poem has more than one speaker. As you prepare your readings, think about each speaker. Make sure that your reading suggests the speaker's attitude, age, and mood. Practice your readings several times and then present them to the class.

2. "To Satch" and "Dorlan's Home-Walk" both refer to the sport that has been called "the great American pastime"— baseball. Why do you think people like to write about baseball? What is it about that sport that captures people's imaginations? What is most exciting about it? In a small group, discuss the sports that you find most interesting. List a few details that could be mentioned in a poem about each sport.

3. With a partner compare and contrast two of the poems in this unit. You may want to create a chart like the one below to help you record the poems' similarities and differences. Feel free to add other categories that come to mind.

	Name of First Poem	Name of Second Poem
Name of Poet		
Topic of Poem		
Identity of Speaker		
Speaker's Attitude		
Monologue or Dialogue?		
Narrative? (Yes or No)		
Setting		

WRITE A POEM OF YOUR CHOICE

In this unit you have learned that poets use different kinds of speakers in their poems and that some poems are monologues and some are dialogues. You also have learned that some poems are narratives that tell stories from a first-person or third-person point of view. In this exercise you will write a poem that uses some or all of the techniques that you have learned in this unit.

Follow these steps to write your poem. If you have questions about the writing process, refer to Using the Writing Process on page 235.

- Assemble and review the work you did for all the writing exercises in this unit: 1) lists of animals and objects that could be used as speakers of poems, 2) sentence stems that explain why you would like or dislike being two particular speakers, 3) a poem that is a monologue or a dialogue, 4) a narrative poem that describes the monologue or dialogue.
- Using the following questions, decide what kind of poem to write:
  1. What do I want my poem to be about? (a person? a place? a thing? a feeling? a situation? an activity?)
  2. Who will be the speaker or speakers in my poem? (real people? imaginary characters? objects? animals?)
  3. What type of poem will I write? (a monologue? a dialogue? a narrative poem?)
  4. Will I use the first-person or third-person point of view?
  5. What kind of mood will my poem convey? (friendly? humorous? cheerful? angry? frightening? confused?)
- When you have made all your decisions, write your poem. Make it as long or short as necessary, depending on the type of poem it is.

- When you have finished, ask a classmate to read your poem aloud so you can listen for places where it isn't clear or where it doesn't have the sound or meaning you intended. Make any changes that you feel are necessary.
- Proofread your poem for spelling and grammar errors. Then make a final copy of it. If you'd like, read your poem aloud to your classmates. Then save it in your writing portfolio.

Sensory Images and Concrete Language

INTRODUCTION

*ABOUT THE
LESSONS*

You know that you have five senses: sight, hearing, smell, taste, and touch. It is through these senses that you experience the world around you. One of the goals of many poets is to create or recreate memorable sensory experiences for their readers. To create these experiences, they paint pictures that appeal to the senses and use exact words to describe the details.

As you read the poems in Group 1, you will examine the ways in which poets use sensory details and concrete language to create striking images. As you read the poems in Group 2, you will see how sensory images and concrete language help create particular moods.

WRITING: ANALYZING A SENSORY EXPERIENCE

Throughout this unit you will be learning how poets appeal to their readers' senses in order to create memorable experiences. At the end of the unit, you will write a description using sensory details. Follow these steps to help you get started:

- In certain situations everyone is bombarded with sights, sounds, smells, tastes, textures, and temperatures—maybe not all at once but within a short period of time. For example, when you travel on a bus or a plane, you see your fellow passengers, you hear the vehicle's engine, you smell and sometimes even taste the exhaust fumes, and you feel the hardness or softness of the seat. Make a list of at least three situations that you have experienced with all or most of your senses. Next to each, list the senses that you used.
- Think about how you felt emotionally as you experienced each situation. List your emotions next to each situation.
- Save your list. You will use it throughout the writing exercises in this unit.

ABOUT THIS POET

Langston Hughes (1902–1967) was born in Joplin, Missouri. He spent much of his childhood in Kansas with his grandmother, however, because his parents were separated. He began writing at an early age; in fact, his first poem, "A Negro Speaks of Rivers," was published when Hughes was only 19 years old. After high school he attended Columbia University in New York City for one year but then decided to travel the world instead of continuing his education. Hughes became a worker on merchant ships, an occupation that allowed him to visit Europe and Africa.

In this job and in later ones—such as janitor, farmer, cook, and doorman—he continued to write. While he was a busboy at a New York restaurant, he placed some of his poems on the poet Vachel Lindsay's table. Lindsay, who was in the middle of a poetry-reading tour, read the poems at his next reading and launched Hughes's literary career.

Hughes became an important figure in the exciting artistic movement of the 1920s known as the Harlem Renaissance. He is remembered for his poetry, short stories, novels, plays, songs, and even a newspaper column. Some say that you can feel the rhythms of jazz and blues in his poetry. Much of his writing depicts the indignities suffered by the African-American community in the United States, but it also expresses hopes for a future in which all races will get along.

Hughes is known for his poetry collections *The Weary Blues* (1926), *The Dream Keeper* (1932), and *Montage of a Dream Deferred* (1951).

Late in life he encouraged budding young writers. He founded three theaters, held poetry readings in universities around the country, and continued to write about the changing experiences of the nation's African Americans.

AS YOU READ   As you read each poem in this unit, ask yourself the following questions:

- To which senses do the details in this poem appeal?
- What mental picture, or image, do these details create?
- How do the poem's images create a particular mood?

My Mother Pieced Quilts

by Teresa Palomo Acosta

ABOUT THE SELECTION

Teresa Palomo Acosta (1949–   ) is a native of Texas. Much of the inspiration for her poetry has come from the stories her grandfather told her about his childhood in Mexico. Acosta attended the University of Texas and Columbia University. She wrote the poem "My Mother Pieced Quilts" as part of a college writing assignment.

they were just meant as covers
in winter
as weapons
against pounding january winds

but it was just that every morning I awoke to these
october ripened canvases
passed my hand across their cloth faces
and began to wonder how you pieced
all these together
these strips of gentle communion cotton and flannel
    nightgowns
wedding organdies
dime store velvets

how you shaped patterns square and oblong and round
positioned
balanced
then cemented them
with your thread
a steel needle
a thimble

how the thread darted in and out
galloping along the frayed edges, tucking them in
as you did us at night
oh how you stretched and turned and re-arranged
your michigan spring faded curtain pieces
my father's santa fe work shirt
the summer denims, the tweeds of fall

in the evening you sat at your canvas
—our cracked linoleum floor the drawing board
me lounging on your arm
and you staking out the plan:
whether to put the lilac purple of easter against the red
    plaid of winter-going
into-spring
whether to mix a yellow with blue and white and paint the
corpus christi noon when my father held your hand
whether to shape a five-point star from the
somber black silk you wore to grandmother's funeral

you were the river current
carrying the roaring notes
forming them into pictures of a little boy reclining
a swallow flying
you were the caravan master at the reins
driving your threaded needle artillery across the mosaic
    cloth bridges
delivering yourself in separate testimonies.

oh mother you plunged me sobbing and laughing
into our past
into the river crossing at five
into the spinach fields
into the plainview cotton rows
into tuberculosis wards
into braids and muslin dresses
sewn hard and taut to withstand the thrashings of twenty-
    five years

stretched out they lay
armed/ready/shouting/celebrating

knotted with love
the quilts sing on

That Was Summer

by Marci Ridlon

ABOUT THE SELECTION

Marci Ridlon specializes in writing poetry that captures the joy of childhood. Her poems are enjoyed by young audiences as well as adults. Anyone who can recall childhood summers can appreciate the feelings that this cheerful poem recreates.

Have you ever smelled summer?
Sure you have.
Remember that time
when you were tired of running
or doing nothing much
and you were hot
and you flopped right down on the ground?
Remember how the warm soil smelled
and the grass?
That was summer.

Remember that time
when the storm blew up quick
and you stood under a ledge
and watched the rain till it stopped
and when it stopped
you walked out again to the sidewalk,
the quiet sidewalk?
Remember how the pavement smelled—
all steamy warm and wet?
That was summer.

Remember that time
when you were trying to climb
higher in the tree
and you didn't know how
and your foot was hurting in the fork
but you were holding tight
to the branch?
Remember how the bark smelled then
all dusty dry, but nice?
That was summer.

If you try very hard,
can you remember that time
when you played outside all day
and you came home for dinner
and had to take a bath right away,
right away?
It took you a long time to pull
your shirt over your head.
Do you remember smelling the sunshine?
That was summer.

Daybreak in Alabama

by Langston Hughes

ABOUT THE SELECTION

Langston Hughes (1902–1967) had many talents. He wrote poetry, short stories, novels, plays, and autobiographical sketches. He became a voice for African Americans and spoke against all forms of racism and prejudice. Although he experienced racism firsthand, he maintained a hopeful attitude toward race relations in the United States. In this poem he combines striking images and a powerful theme. For more information about Langston Hughes, see About This Poet at the beginning of this unit.

When I get to be a composer
I'm gonna write me some music about
Daybreak in Alabama
And I'm gonna put the purtiest songs in it
Rising out of the ground like a swamp mist
And falling out of heaven like soft dew.
I'm gonna put some tall tall trees in it
And the scent of pine needles
And the smell of red clay after rain
And long red necks
And poppy colored faces
And big brown arms
And the field daisy eyes
Of black and white black white black people
And I'm gonna put white hands
And black hands and brown and yellow hands
And red clay earth hands in it

Touching everybody with kind fingers
And touching each other natural as dew
In that dawn of music when I
Get to be a composer
And write about daybreak
In Alabama.

Vacant House

by Jeanne DeLamarter Bonnette

ABOUT THE SELECTION

In the following poem Jeanne DeLamarter Bonnette combines her powers of observation with her own imagination to describe what she sees when she looks at—and beyond—a vacant house.

Beside the old earth-colored
adobe house haphazard on the ground
whose doors have vanished
and whose window frames are empty
wherein tumbleweeds have hidden at last
from the wind in corners

the rusty upside-down cars
lie like dark wing-folded shells
of beetles on the dry earth.

Majestic cottonwoods
rise above the corral
with no boy to throw a rope
over a low-hanging branch,
no man to lean a rake
against the great trunk,
no woman to stand in the shade,
her apron fluttering as she holds
a hand over her eyes
against the brilliance.

The echo of horses stamping
has long ago faded from the air
and now only the crows
perch high in the upper boughs
to scold the ghosts
Of those who once were here
working, belonging.

In Winter

by Robert Wallace

ABOUT THE SELECTION

Robert Wallace (1932–   ), born in Springfield, Missouri, attended both Harvard University in the United States and Cambridge University in England. He has written several books of poems while teaching English at various colleges and universities in the United States. Even if you have never seen the ocean, you probably will be able to get a clear picture of it from the poem you are about to read.

It is hard, inland,
   in winter,
when the fields are motionless in snow,

to remember waves, to remember
   the wide, sloshing
immensity

of the Atlantic, continuous,
   green in the cold, taking snow
or rain into itself,

to realize the endurance
   of the tilting bell buoy
(hour by hour, years

through) that clangs, clangs,
   leaning
with the rocking waters, miles

from land; even in storm and
   night-howling
snow, wet, red, flashing

to mark the channel. Some
   things
are, even if no one comes.

The Tom-Cat

by Don Marquis

ABOUT THE SELECTION

Don Marquis (1878–1937) was best known for his humorous columns in the *New York Evening Sun,* in which he spoke as a cockroach named archy and an alley-cat named mehitabel who used Marquis's typewriter at night. (The animals couldn't reach the typewriter key that prints capital letters.) In the following poem Marquis paints a picture of an ordinary tom-cat that is quite different from the soft, cuddly image that others often imagine.

At midnight in the alley
  A Tom-Cat comes to wail,
And he chants the hate of a million years
  As he swings his snaky tail.

Malevolent,[1] bony, brindled,[2]
  Tiger and devil and bard,[3]
His eyes are coals from the middle of Hell
  And his heart is black and hard.

---

[1] evil

[2] having a gray color and streaked with a darker color

[3] poet

He twists and crouches and capers
    And bares his curved sharp claws,
And he sings to the stars of the jungle nights
    Ere[4] cities were, or laws.

Beast from a world primeval,[5]
    He and his leaping clan,
When the blotched red moon leers[6] over the
    roofs,
    Give voice to their scorn of man.

He will lie on a rug tomorrow
    And lick his silky fur,
And veil[7] the brute in his yellow eyes
    And play he's tame, and purr.

But at midnight in the alley
    He will crouch again and wail,
And beat the time for his demon's song
    With the swing of his demon's tail.

---

[4] before

[5] found in the earliest of times

[6] looks as if intending to do evil deeds

[7] to cover up or disguise something

Girl with 'Cello

by May Sarton

ABOUT THE SELECTION

May Sarton (1912–1995) was born in Belgium and moved to the United States with her parents in 1916. She is known for both her poetry and her novels, and in 1959 she wrote her autobiography, *I Know a Phoenix.* Sarton was a poet in residence and guest lecturer at several colleges throughout her life. She continued to write poetry and prose until just a few months before her death. As you read this poem, try to imagine how you would feel if you heard the sound of a cello in your living room on a winter night.

There had been no such music here until
A girl came in from falling dark and snow
To bring into this house her glowing 'cello
As if some silent, magic animal.

She sat, head bent, her long hair all aspill
Over the breathing wood, and drew the bow.
There had been no such music here until
A girl came in from falling dark and snow.

And she drew out that sound so like a wail,
A rich dark suffering joy, as if to show
All that a wrist holds and that fingers know
When they caress a magic animal.
There had been no such music here until
A girl came in from falling dark and snow.

UNDERSTANDING THE POEMS

Record your answers to these questions in your personal literature notebook. Follow the directions for each group.

GROUP 1

Reread the poems in Group 1 to complete these sentences.

Reviewing the Selection

1. Three things found in nature that are mentioned in "Daybreak in Alabama" are
   a. pine needles, swamp mist, dew.
   b. wind, red clay, hands.
   c. swamp mist, sunsets, brown arms.
   d. poppies, rain, waves.

2. The speaker in "That Was Summer" describes all of these experiences *except*
   a. climbing a tree and smelling its bark.
   b. flopping down on the grass.
   c. smelling the pavement after a summer rain.
   d. lying on the ground and counting the stars.

Interpreting the Selection

3. In "My Mother Pieced Quilts" the way the mother combined the various pieces of cloth to make a quilt is a symbol of her ability to
   a. sew clothes for the members of the family.
   b. save cloth and recycle it.
   c. create a valuable history from different life experiences.
   d. teach others how to sew.

4. The phrase "october ripened canvases" in "My Mother Pieced Quilts" suggests a feeling of
   a. fear.
   b. security and satisfaction.
   c. suspense and intrigue.
   d. decay and death.

Appreciating Poetry

5. In "That Was Summer" what does the speaker describe as "all steamy warm and wet"?
  a. the grass when you flopped down on it
  b. the pavement after a rain storm
  c. the bark of the tree
  d. your shirt as you pulled it over your head

GROUP 2 Reread the poems in Group 2 to complete these sentences.

Reviewing the Selection

6. The events in "Girl with 'Cello" take place in
  a. spring.
  b. summer.
  c. fall.
  d. winter.

7. The details in "Vacant House" suggest that the house used to be a
  a. center for storing used cars.
  b. fancy home owned by a wealthy farmer.
  c. small, simple home on the prairie.
  d. busy place for travelers to stop and eat.

Interpreting the Selection

8. In the poem "In Winter" the attitude of the speaker toward the persistence of the bell buoy is
  a. pity.
  b. respect.
  c. confusion.
  d. anger.

Recognizing How Words Are Used

9. In each stanza of "The Tom-Cat" there are rhyming words at the ends of the
  a. first and second lines.
  b. first and third lines.
  c. second and fourth lines.
  d. first and fourth lines.

Appreciating Poetry

10. In "The Tom-Cat" the speaker compares the cat to all of these creatures except a
   a. snake.
   b. tiger.
   c. devil.
   d. dog.

Now check your answers with your teacher. Study the questions you answered incorrectly. What types of questions were they? Talk with your teacher about ways to work on those skills.

Sensory Images and Concrete Language

Imagine that you just came back from an exciting football game and want to describe it to a friend. In order to recreate your experience, you use the most exact words you can think of to paint a clear picture of what you saw, felt, heard, said, and tasted at the game. By painting as clear a picture as possible, you are helping your friend imagine what it would have felt like to be sitting next to you at the game.

Many poets want to share their experiences with their readers. To do that, they use *sensory images*—words and phrases that create a mental picture by appealing to their readers' senses. For example, a poet who attended the football game might describe the bright clothing of the fans and players, the smell of hot dogs, the taste of hot cocoa, the sound of the fans' cheering, or the cold wind that swept through the stadium. Poets spend a great deal of time deciding on the details that are most important. They work hard to choose just the right words to communicate what they experienced and to convey how those experiences made them feel.

In these lessons you will look at the ways in which poets create effective images in their poems:

- Poets paint mental pictures by using specific, concrete words that appeal to the readers' senses.
- Poets create specific moods in their poems by using clear images.

LESSON 1 SENSORY IMAGES, SENSORY DETAILS, AND CONCRETE LANGUAGE

One of the most important ways in which poetry differs from prose is in its use of *sensory images*—mental pictures created by colorful and exact words and phrases. The colors of a sunset, the feel of the rain, and the smell of a garbage can in summer are all examples of images.

When an image appeals to a particular sense or senses, it is called a *sensory image*. The small details that identify things that your senses experience are called *sensory details*. Many sensory details together can create a sensory image. For example, read this stanza from "That Was Summer." What sensory image do the details paint in your mind? To what senses do these details appeal?

> Remember that time
> When you were trying to climb
> Higher in the tree
> And you didn't know how
> And your foot was hurting in the fork
> But you were holding tight
> To the branch?
> Remember how the bark smelled then—
> All dusty dry, but nice?
> That was summer.

The poet's words help you picture yourself climbing a tree. You feel the painful pinch of the tree's fork squeezing your foot and the rough feel of the bark on your palms as you hold on tight. You smell the bark, "all dusty dry, but nice." Using all these details, you probably can form a mental image of the tree and your hands and feet. The poem uses sensory details that give you a clear image of what it feels like to climb a tree in the summer.

To make an experience seem as real as possible, poets also use concrete language. *Concrete language* refers to words that describe things that readers can experience with their senses. For example, Marci Ridlon uses concrete language in "That Was Summer" to describe the tree bark as "dusty dry." These concrete words help the poet describe something that readers can actually see and feel.

On the other hand, in "Daybreak in Alabama," Langston Hughes uses concrete language to make an imaginary situation seem real. In this poem the speaker is talking about a song that he or she wants to compose. Because readers can't hear this imaginary song, the speaker uses concrete language to describe what it would sound like. Find examples of concrete language in the following lines from the poem:

> And I'm gonna put white hands
> And black hands and brown and yellow hands
> And red clay earth hands in it
> Touching everybody with kind fingers
> And touching each other natural as dew

The poet has chosen words that paint a clear picture in your mind. His concrete language helps you see a combination of different-colored hands in a kind of human bouquet. You feel the "kind fingers" touching each other lightly. The concrete language and sensory details create an extraordinary image that suggests an uplifting, wonderful song.

In "My Mother Pieced Quilts" poet Teresa Palomo Acosta uses both sensory images and concrete language to share the speaker's feelings about her mother. Notice how Acosta has chosen exact words to make the experience seem more real. To which senses do the words in the following lines appeal?

> but it was just that every morning I awoke to these
> october ripened canvases
> passed my hand across their cloth faces
> and began to wonder how you pieced
> all these together
> these strips of gentle communion cotton and flannel
>   nightgowns
> wedding organdies
> dime store velvets

The speaker sees "october ripened canvases" and feels the "cloth faces" of each individual piece of fabric. By specifying that the fabrics are cotton or organdy or velvet, the poet helps readers see and feel the variety of pieces that have been sewn together.

EXERCISE 1

Reread "Daybreak in Alabama." Then use what you have learned in this lesson to answer the following questions:

1. Which sensory details and concrete words in the poem appeal to the reader's sense of sight?

2. Which sensory details and concrete words appeal to the sense of touch?

3. Which sensory details and concrete words appeal to the sense of smell?

Now check your answers with your teacher. Review this part of the lesson if you don't understand why an answer was incorrect.

 WRITING ON YOUR OWN 1

One place in which all of your senses are stimulated is the school lunchroom or cafeteria. In this exercise you will describe a lunchroom experience using sensory details and concrete language. Follow these steps:

- First, make a cluster chart like the one that follows.

ST. ANDREW JUNIOR
SCHOOL LIBRARY

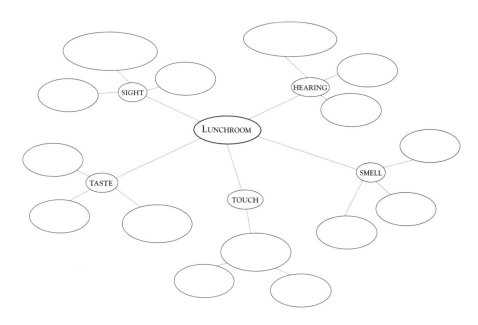

- Next, fill in the chart with details that describe your sensory experiences in the lunchroom. Try to be as specific and concrete as possible. For example, for the *hearing* category, you might write the words *laughing students, clanging silverware,* and *lunchroom attendant's whistle.* Include at least three sensory details for each category.
- Last, use the details that you just listed to write a paragraph describing your lunch time in the cafeteria. Begin with a sentence that identifies the topic of your description and gives readers an idea about your attitude toward it. Continue with at least five other sentences, each discussing what one of your senses perceives.

LESSON 2   IMAGES AND MOOD

Suppose two people went to the same family picnic. One person really enjoyed the picnic—seeing relatives and friends, eating favorite home-cooked dishes, and playing games. Describing the picnic later, he would mention the friendly faces, the delicious potato salad, and the feel of the bat hitting the ball when he made a home run. Another person who attended the picnic might have been in a terrible mood that day. She had wanted to be somewhere else, so she deliberately refused to have fun. Describing the picnic later, she would mention the flies on the food, the warm pop, and the dirt and bruises she got while sliding into first base.

By including different images in their descriptions, these two people would create very different pictures of the same picnic. Reading the first description would make you wish you had been at the picnic. Reading the second would make you glad that you missed it.

Poets often communicate their feelings about a subject just as the picnic-goers might. They use carefully chosen words and images to convey their feelings and to create the same feeling in their readers. In literature that general feeling that the writer creates is called a *mood*.

Read this part of the poem "Vacant House." What mood does it create in you? How do the images help to create that mood?

> Beside the old earth-colored
> adobe house haphazard on the ground
> whose doors have vanished
> and whose window frames are empty
> wherein tumbleweeds have hidden at last
> from the wind in the corners

The mood of the poem is rather sad. All the visual images describe an old abandoned house, probably somewhere in the Southwest, where adobe houses are common. The doors and windows are gone, and tumbleweeds hide from the wind in the corners of the empty house. If you continue to read the poem, you will see that all the images work together to support the somber mood.

In "The Tom-Cat" poet Don Marquis uses strong images to create a menacing mood. Read this stanza from the poem to find images that should make you frightened of the cat:

> Beast from a world primeval,
>   He and his leaping clan,
> When the blotched red moon leers over the
>   roofs,
>   Give voice to their scorn of man.

The poet describes the cat as a beast who is part of a leaping clan, suggesting that it is wild and probably dangerous. The mention of a red moon leering, or looking in an evil way, adds to the frightening image. You can almost hear the screeching of the cats as they give "voice to their scorn of man." These images together create a chilling mood.

Also notice the poet's choice of words. He uses the word *beast* instead of *animal*. He chooses *leaping* instead of *jumping* and *clan* instead of *family*. Each of these words adds to the scary mood. The poet has chosen words not only for their meaning, called their *denotation*, but also for the feelings they give, called their *connotation*.

In the poem "In Winter" Robert Wallace chooses a different image to convey the mood. The poem's mood is one of respect for the endurance of the lone bell buoy that does its job despite the harsh winds and cold of the ocean winter. All the accompanying images—the cold green water taking in snow, the clang of the lonely bell, the howling wind—combine to emphasize the perseverance of the buoy.

EXERCISE 2

Reread "Girl with 'Cello" and then use what you have learned in this lesson to answer the following questions:

1. There are several interesting images in "Girl with 'Cello." In your opinion, which is the best, most memorable image? What other images are connected with the image you chose?

2. How would you describe the mood that those images create when they are all combined? Is the overall mood joyful, sad, awesome, magical, or thoughtful—or could it be described in a different way?

Now check your answers with your teacher. Review this part of the lesson if you don't understand why an answer was incorrect.

WRITING ON YOUR OWN 2

In this exercise you will think about experiences that you reacted to with strong feelings, and you will list images that would communicate those feelings. Follow these steps:

- List times in your life when you felt strong emotions—for example, fear, happiness, surprise, or excitement. For ideas, review the list of experiences that appealed to your senses, which you drew up at the beginning of this unit. Add any other experiences that you can think of.
- Choose three experiences and make a note card for each one. At the top of each card, identify your mood, the way you felt at that time.
- Now list at least three images that you could use to communicate how you felt. For example, if you were once afraid of a dog, you might list the dog's huge, sharp teeth grinning at you, its stiff-legged stance, and its fierce growl.

DISCUSSION GUIDES

1. With a small group of classmates, choose a favorite holiday. Then discuss and record the images that you associate with that holiday. For example, for the Fourth of July, you may think of the images of fireworks against a night sky, a parade with marching bands and floats, and the American flag waving. What feelings do these images create in you? After your group has made a list of at least five images and has discussed the moods that the images create, share your list with other groups in the class. If you chose the same holiday as another group, are any of your group's images similar to theirs? Are the moods similar?

2. Don Marquis, the poet who wrote "The Tom-Cat," sees the cat in his poem as dangerous and perhaps evil. Do you think that this view of cats makes sense, or do you think cats have been unfairly portrayed in this poem? Discuss the reasons someone might think that a cat is a little frightening. Then give your opinion of cats in general. If possible, find out how cats have been viewed through the ages and give a short report to the class.

3. "Girl with 'Cello" has a thoughtful, quiet mood, in keeping with the instrument that the girl is playing. Suppose that in a new poem, you changed the instrument that the girl plays. How would the use of a different instrument change the mood of the poem? With a group of classmates, identify the mood of a poem in which the girl plays each of these instruments: tuba, banjo, accordion, guitar, violin, kazoo, drums, and saxophone. If you'd like, you may add other instruments as well.

WRITE A DESCRIPTIVE POEM

In this unit you have learned how poets use sensory details, concrete language, and imagery to describe experiences and create moods. Now you will write a poem about a place or an experience using the same techniques.

Follow these steps to write your poem. If you have questions about the writing process, refer to Using the Writing Process (page 235).

- Assemble and review the work you did for all the writing exercises in this unit: 1) a list of experiences or situations that appealed to several senses and the feelings connected with each experience, 2) a cluster map and paragraph describing your sensory experiences in a lunchroom, 3) three note cards containing images that communicate your mood in an emotion-filled situation.
- Think of a place or a past experience that you feel very strongly about. It can be one of the experiences that you listed in previous exercises, or you can choose a new experience.
- List the ways the experience affected each of your senses. (If you wish, use a cluster chart like the one you created earlier to organize your ideas.) Think of images that could communicate your experiences and feelings.
- Now use your notes to write a poem that describes your chosen place or experience. Be sure to include images that will make your readers understand your mood and feel it themselves. Make your language as concrete and specific as possible. Choose words based on what they mean as well as how they will make your readers feel.
- Read your poem aloud to a classmate. Ask him or her to identify the mood of the piece. If your classmate has trouble, consider adding more images, using words that are more specific and concrete, or replacing dull words with strong ones. Make any changes necessary.
- Proofread your poem for spelling and grammar errors. Then make a final copy to save in your writing portfolio.

Sounds in Poetry

INTRODUCTION

ABOUT THE LESSONS

Sounds are important in poetry. Just as much as words do, sounds help a poet express a poem's meaning. A skillful poet, therefore, chooses individual words as much for their sounds as for their meanings. In each of the lessons in this unit, you will focus on different aspects of sound in poetry. In Lesson 1 you will listen for the rhythms of poems—their patterns of stressed and unstressed syllables. In Lesson 2 you will look for rhyming sounds—the matching sounds at the ends of words. In Lesson 3 you will focus on repeated con-sonant and vowel sounds and other sound effects.

WRITING: USING SOUNDS EFFECTIVELY IN A POEM

Poets regularly use specific rhythms, rhymes, and other sound techniques to make their poems effective. As you learn about these sound techniques, you will practice applying them in your own writing. Then, at the end of the unit, you will write a poem that uses the sounds of words to emphasize their meaning. You can begin thinking about topics to write about by following these steps:

- Many machines make specific sounds. For example, think of the different sounds that a vacuum cleaner, a car engine, and a computer keyboard make. Could these sounds be suggested by any specific words? For example, might a car engine purr or the keys on a computer key-board click? Make a list of machines whose sounds you could suggest with words.
- Many animals and weather conditions also produce sounds. Their sounds often are described by words such as *roar, honk, scream, hiss, whoosh,* and *whistle.* Make a list of several other sounds that are made by animals or weather conditions.

- Some activities, such as cross-country skiing and ice skating, involve smooth and steady motions. Other activities, such as playing basketball and walking in a crowded store, require many starts and stops. Sentences or lines of poems can suggest the pace and rhythm of different activities. Make a list of activities with definite paces or rhythms that you might suggest through your words.
- Save your lists of words and activities that suggest different sounds and rhythms. You will use them in the final writing exercise of this unit.

ABOUT THIS POET

John Ciardi was a teacher, critic, speaker, translator, and poet known for his clear, graceful writing. He was born in Boston, Massachusetts, in 1916, after his parents had immigrated to the United States from Italy. After he had become known for his own poetry, Ciardi received praise for translating into English an epic poem called *The Divine Comedy* by the Italian poet Dante.

Ciardi graduated from Tufts College, earned a master's degree at the University of Michigan, and published his first book of poetry in 1940. He began teaching college at the University of Kansas City, but when the United States entered World War II, he enlisted in the Air Force and served as an aerial gunner.

Not long after his return to teaching, Ciardi became a professor at Harvard University and then at Rutgers, where he taught until 1961. In addition, from 1956 to 1977 he served as poetry editor of *Saturday Review* magazine. At the same time, he was translating *The Divine Comedy*, writing poetry and criticism that influenced many other poets, and producing poetry for children as well. His 1960 book *How Does a Poem Mean?* is still used as a college textbook. He eventually produced about 40 books in all.

During the 1950s Ciardi took his love of poetry and words beyond the classroom and onto television. Through his weekly television series, and later on TV specials, he shared his enjoyment of literature with a wide audience. During the last ten years of his life, he appeared regularly on National Public Radio to discuss poetry and the history of words.

Ciardi died in 1986 at his home in New Jersey, where he and his wife had reared their three children.

| **AS YOU READ** | As you read each of the poems in this unit, ask yourself these questions about the way the poem sounds:

- Do the lines of this poem sound like normal conversation? If not, how are they different?
- Where do I hear rhymes in this poem?
- Where do I hear the repetition of sounds other than rhyming endings?

Indians

by Ophelia Rivas

**ABOUT THE
SELECTION**

Ophelia Rivas (1956–   ) is of Tohono O'odham heritage.
When she was in eighth grade, she entered a creative-writing
contest sponsored by the Bureau of Indian Affairs. The poem
she wrote, entitled "Indians," won the contest and was published in 1971. It was later included in the collection *Rising
Voices: Writings of Young Native Americans.*

Indians are native people
   here before the Pilgrims came
   here before Columbus came
   here before the Vikings came
Yet, we are treated
As though we don't belong here
Indians are native people
   here before the Pilgrims came
   here before Columbus came
   here before the Vikings came
Yet, we are treated
As though we just got here.

Crossing

by Philip Booth

ABOUT THE SELECTION

Philip Booth (1925–   ) grew up in New Hampshire and Maine and graduated from Dartmouth, the college where his father taught. Booth himself also taught at Dartmouth and other New England colleges before joining the faculty at Syracuse University. He has published several books of poetry and is noted for his short, simple-looking poems.

In "Crossing," Booth describes a long freight train rolling through a railroad crossing. He refers to many railroad lines, such as the B&O, the Frisco, and the Erie and Wabash. Among the railway cars he mentions are the *boxcar,* a freight car with sides and top; the *gondola*, a freight car with low sides and no top; the *hopper*, a freight car whose bottom opens for unloading cargo; and the *caboose*, the crew's car, which usually is placed at the end of the train.

STOP   LOOK   LISTEN
as gate stripes swing down,
  count the cars hauling distance
    upgrade through town:
     warning whistle, bellclang,
     engine eating steam,
     engineer waving,
      a fast-freight dream:
      B&M boxcar,
       boxcar again,
        Frisco gondola,

eight-nine-ten,
  Erie and Wabash,
    Seaboard, U.P.,
      Pennsy tankcar,
twenty-two, three,
  Phoebe Snow, B&O,
thirty-four, five,
  Santa Fe cattle
    shipped alive,
      red cars, yellow cars,
        orange cars, black,
          Youngstown steel
            down to Mobile
              on Rock Island track,
fifty-nine, sixty,
  hoppers of coke,
    Anaconda copper,
  hotbox smoke,
eighty-eight,
  red-ball freight,
    Rio Grande,
      Nickel Plate,
        Hiawatha,
          Lackawanna,
            rolling fast
              and loose,
ninety-seven,
  coal car,
    boxcar,
      CABOOSE!

Annabel Lee

by Edgar Allan Poe

ABOUT THE SELECTION

Edgar Allan Poe (1809–1849) was one of the most influential writers in American literature. He wrote memorable horror stories, the first modern detective stories, reviews of other writers' works, and musical and emotional poems. "Annabel Lee," one of the last poems Poe wrote in his short life, concerns one of his favorite themes, the death of a beautiful woman.

It was many and many a year ago,
    In a kingdom by the sea,
That a maiden there lived whom you may know
    By the name of Annabel Lee;
And this maiden she lived with no other thought
    Than to love and be loved by me.

She was a child and *I* was a child,
    In this kingdom by the sea,
But we loved with a love that was more than love—
    I and my Annabel Lee—
With a love that the wingèd seraphs[1] of Heaven
    Coveted her and me.

---
[1] angels

And this was the reason that, long ago,
   In this kingdom by the sea,
A wind blew out of a cloud by night
   Chilling my Annabel Lee;
So that her high-born kinsmen came
   And bore her away from me,
To shut her up in a sepulchre[2]
   In this kingdom by the sea.

The angels, not half so happy in Heaven,
   Went envying her and me:—
Yes! that was the reason (as all men know,
   In this kingdom by the sea)
That the wind came out of the cloud chilling
   And killing my Annabel Lee.

But our love it was stronger by far than the love
   Of those who were older than we—
   Of many far wiser than we—
And neither the angels in Heaven above
   Nor the demons down under the sea
Can ever dissever[3] my soul from the soul
   Of the beautiful Annabel Lee:

For the moon never beams without bringing me dreams
   Of the beautiful Annabel Lee;
And the stars never rise but I feel the bright eyes
   Of the beautiful Annabel Lee:
And so all the night-tide, I lie down by the side
Of my darling, my darling, my life and my bride
   In her sepulchre there by the sea—
   In her tomb by the side of the sea.

---

[2] burial vault

[3] separate

Bears

by Arthur Guiterman

ABOUT THE SELECTION

Arthur Guiterman (1871–1943) was an extremely productive writer, best known for his humorous verse and ballads on American history. In addition to his many poems, Guiterman wrote nonfiction articles and the *librettos*, or words, for light and classical operas. Here's a hint for getting the full enjoyment out of "Bears": don't worry about the meaning of the unfamiliar words; the important ideas are in the simple ones.

High up among the mountains, through a lovely grove of
    cedars
    They came on ferny forest ways and trails that lift and
        wind,
The bears of many ranges under celebrated leaders
    Assembling in a congress for the weal[1] of all their kind.

    Black bears, brown bears,
    Sober bears and clown bears,
Chubby bears and tubby bears and bears austerely planned,
    Bears of mild benignity,[2]
    Bears of simple dignity,
Coming to the Council of the Bruins of the Land.

---

[1] well-being; prosperity

[2] kind and gentle action

A most tremendous Grizzly was Exalted Cockalorum;[3]
    He didn't need a gavel for his paw was hard and square.
The meeting was conducted with unparalleled decorum,[4]
    For no one ever questioned the decisions of the Chair.

    Fat bears, lean bears,
    Muddy bears and clean bears,
Tawny bears and brawny bears and bears in heavy coats,
    Bears of perspicacity,[5]
    Bears of much loquacity,[6]
Rumbling ghostly noises in their tummies and their throats.

They argued that their greatest need was more and better
      honey,
    That berries ought to propagate[7] in every vacant space;
They voted that the Teddy Bear was anything but funny,
    Demanding his suppression as a Libel on the Race.

    Dark bears, light bears,
    Stupid bears and bright bears,
Gabby bears and flabby bears and bears of force and will,
    Bears of deep humility,
    Bears of marked ability,
Dealing with Conditions with extraordinary skill.

---

[3] an unimportant person who brags a great deal with unreasonably high self-esteem

[4] fitting or appropriate behavior

[5] keen understanding

[6] talkativeness

[7] multiply; grow

Their orators orated on the laxity[8] of morals
  Contrasted with the beauty of the early forest den;
They favored arbitration[9] for the settlement of quarrels
  And instant abolition[10] of the armaments of men.

Weak bears, strong bears,
  Proper bears and wrong bears,
Eager bears and meager bears and bears morose and glum,
  Locally admired bears,
  Splendidly inspired bears,
Working for the Future and the Bear that Is to Come.

They settled mighty matters with miraculous discern-
      ment,[11]
  They voted a Committee on the Stinginess of Bees,
They voted for a banquet and immediate adjournment
  And rolled away like shadows through the vistas of the
      trees.

  Red bears, gray bears,
  Gloomy bears and gay bears,
Ambling off in bevies[12] down the boulder-bordered run,
  Bears in sweet amenity,[13]
  Bears in calm serenity,
Sure that what is voted for is just as good as done.

---

[8] looseness

[9] coming to an agreement by accepting the opinion of a third party

[10] ending; doing away with

[11] use of good judgment

[12] groups

[13] agreeableness

The Shark

by John Ciardi

ABOUT THE SELECTION

John Ciardi was born in 1916 and died in 1986. He was a college teacher, a magazine editor, and a poet who wrote for adults and children. For more information about Ciardi, see About This Poet at the beginning of this unit. "The Shark" is one of Ciardi's lighter poems, which reflects his keen sense of humor.

My dear, let me tell you about the shark.
Though his eyes are bright, his thought is dark.
He's quiet—that speaks well of him.
So does the fact that he can swim.
But though he swims without a sound,
Wherever he swims he looks around
With those two bright eyes and that one dark thought.
He has only one but he thinks it a lot.
And the thought he thinks but can never complete
Is his long dark thought of something to eat.
Most anything does. And I have to add
That when he eats his manners are bad.
He's a gulper, a ripper, a snatcher, a grabber.
Yes, his manners are drab. But his thought is drabber.
That one dark thought he can never complete
Of something—anything—somehow to eat.

Be careful where you swim, my sweet.

Wilbur Wright and Orville Wright

by Rosemary and Stephen Vincent Benét

ABOUT THE SELECTION

Rosemary Carr Benét (1898–1962), was a correspondent for *The London Daily Mail* and the *Chicago Tribune.* Her husband, Stephen Vincent Benét (1898–1943) was a major American poet and fiction writer whose greatest works concerned important events in American history. He received the Pulitzer Prize for poetry in 1929 for his epic poem on the Civil War, *John Brown's Body,* and again in 1944 for *Western Star,* about the settling of the Plymouth and Jamestown colonies. In 1933 the couple wrote *A Book of Americans*, a collection of poems about people in American history, including Wilbur and Orville Wright, the pioneers of flight.

Said Orville Wright to Wilbur Wright,
"These birds are very trying.
I'm sick of hearing them cheep-cheep
About the fun of flying.
A bird has feathers, it is true.
That much I freely grant.
But, must that stop us, W?"
Said Wilbur Wright, "It shan't."

And so they built a glider, first,
And then they built another.
—There never were two brothers more
Devoted to each other.
They ran a dusty little shop
For bicycle-repairing,
And bought each other soda-pop
And praised each other's daring.

They glided here, they glided there,
They sometimes skinned their noses,
—For learning how to rule the air
Was not a bed of roses—
But each would murmur, afterward,
While patching up his bro.
"Are we discouraged, W?"
"Of course we are not, O!"

And finally, at Kitty Hawk
In Nineteen-Three (let's cheer it!),
The first real airplane really flew
With Orville there to steer it!
—And kingdoms may forget their kings
And dogs forget their bites,
But, not till Man forgets his wings,
Will men forget the Wrights.

We Real Cool

by Gwendolyn Brooks

ABOUT THE SELECTION

Gwendolyn Brooks (1917–   ) was the first African American ever to receive a Pulitzer Prize. She won the prize for her second book of poetry, *Annie Allen,* which tells about a black girl growing up in America during World War II. Brooks grew up in Chicago and set many of her poems there—although "We Real Cool" could describe defiant young people who live anywhere.

The Pool Players.
Seven at the Golden Shovel.

> We real cool. We
> Left school. We
>
> Lurk late. We
> Strike straight. We
>
> Sing sin. We
> Thin gin. We
>
> Jazz[1] June. We
> Die soon.

---

[1] add excitement to something

The Flower-Fed Buffaloes

by Vachel Lindsay

ABOUT THE SELECTION

Vachel Lindsay (1879–1931) was an American poet whose works are usually marked by strong rhythms. His favorite topics included nature, baseball, the circus, and politicians. Since he felt that poetry should be performed, he included stage directions in several of his poems. "The Flower-Fed Buffaloes" shows Lindsay's interest in nature and the American experience.

The flower-fed buffaloes of the spring
In the days of long ago,
Ranged where the locomotives sing
And the prairie flowers lie low:—
The tossing, blooming, perfumed grass
Is swept away by the wheat,
Wheels and wheels and wheels spin by
In the spring that still is sweet.
But the flower-fed buffaloes of the spring
Left us, long ago.
They gore no more, they bellow no more,
They trundle around the hills no more:—
With the Blackfeet, lying low,
With the Pawnees,[1] lying low,
Lying low.

---

[1] Native American peoples of the Great Plains and the West

Sea Fever

by John Masefield

ABOUT THE SELECTION

John Masefield (1878–1967) was England's poet laureate—its best poet—from 1930 until his death. In addition to poetry, he wrote novels, plays, and literary criticism. Before beginning his writing career, however, Masefield was a sailor. He apprenticed as a sailor when he was only 13 years old and spent the next four years at sea. The sea and its travelers was a favorite topic of his writing, as is evidenced in "Sea Fever."

I must go down to the seas again, to the lonely sea and the
    sky,
And all I ask is a tall ship and a star to steer her by;
And the wheel's kick and the wind's song and the white
    sail's shaking,
And a gray mist on the sea's face and a gray dawn breaking.

I must go down to the seas again, for the call of the running
    tide
Is a wild call and a clear call that may not be denied;
And all I ask is a windy day with the white clouds flying,
And the flung spray and the brown spume,[1] and the sea
    gulls crying.

---

[1] foam on a liquid, as on the sea

I must go down to the seas again, to the vagrant gypsy life,
To the gull's way and the whale's way where the wind's like
   a whetted[2] knife;
And all I ask is a merry yarn from a laughing fellow-rover,
And quiet sleep and a sweet dream when the long trick's[3]
   over.

---

[2] sharpened

[3] a turn of duty, as at the helm of a ship

A Legend of Paul Bunyan

by Arthur S. Bourinot

ABOUT THE SELECTION

Paul Bunyan is a giant woodsman in American tall tales. He was said to have performed such marvelous feats as changing the landscape by hitching Babe, his giant blue ox, to a river and having her pull the river straight. It is unclear where tales of Paul Bunyan began; stories about him first appeared in print in 1910. In his poem "A Legend of Paul Bunyan" Arthur Bourinot describes the mythical giant on an evening walk.

He came,
striding
over the mountain,
the moon slung on his back,
like a pack,
a great pine
stuck on his shoulder
swayed as he walked,
as he talked
to his blue ox
Babe;
a huge, looming shadow
of a man,
clad
in a mackinaw coat,
his logger's shirt
open at the throat

and the great mane of hair
matching
meeting
the locks of night,
the smoke from his cauldron[1] pipe
a cloud on the moon
and his laugh
rolled through the mountains
like thunder
on a summer night
while the lightning of his smile
split the heavens
asunder.[2]
His blue ox, Babe,
pawed the ground
till the earth
trembled
and shook
and a high cliff
toppled and fell:
and Babe's bellow
was fellow
to the echo
of Bunyan's laughter;
and then
with one step
he was in the next valley
dragging the moon after,
the stars
tangled,
spangled[3]

---

[1] a large vessel or pot, such as a kettle

[2] apart; into pieces

[3] sparkled

in the branches of the great pine.
And as he left,
he whistled in the dark
like a far off train
blowing for a crossing
and plainly heard
were the plodding grunts
of Babe, the blue ox,
trying
to keep pace
from hill to hill,
and then, the sounds
fading,
dying,
were lost
in the churn of night,
and all was still.

UNDERSTANDING THE POEMS

Record your answers to these questions in your personal literature notebook. Follow the directions for each group.

GROUP 1 Reread the poems in Group 1 to complete these sentences.

Reviewing the Selection

1. In "Crossing" the last car on the train is a
   a. coal car.
   b. caboose.
   c. hopper.
   d. gondola.

2. The speaker in "Annabel Lee" mourns his love because
   a. she left him for another man.
   b. her relatives separated them.
   c. she was buried alive.
   d. a cold wind made her ill, and she died.

Interpreting the Selection

3. A reader can be sure that the speaker in "Indians"
   a. has great respect for Columbus.
   b. would have welcomed the Pilgrims.
   c. considers Columbus and the Pilgrims the newcomers.
   d. thinks the Vikings came to America after Columbus did.

Recognizing How Words Are Used

4. Of the following lines from "Annabel Lee," the one that best shows repetition of the /h/ sound is
   a. "Went envying her and me."
   b. "With a love that the wingèd seraphs of Heaven."
   c. "So that her high-born kinsmen came."
   d. "The angels, not half so happy in Heaven."

Appreciating Poetry

5. Certain lines in "Crossing" are printed in darker type because in all of them the speaker is
a. making very important statements.
b. explaining where the crossing is.
c. counting the cars that pass through the crossing.
d. expressing his or her personal feelings.

GROUP 2   Reread the poems in Group 2 to complete these sentences.

Reviewing the Selection

6. The speaker in "The Shark" admires the shark for
a. its ability to swim.
b. its good manners when eating.
c. its one dark thought.
d. all of the above.

7. The main idea of "The Shark" is that a shark
a. has bad manners when it eats.
b. can swim quietly.
c. is always hungry.
d. swims faster than most people.

Interpreting the Selection

8. In "Bears" the speaker's attitude toward the bears is one of
a. fear.
b. awe.
c. amusement.
d. hatred.

Recognizing How Words Are Used

9. In "Wilbur Wright and Orville Wright" the phrase *a bed of roses* means
a. "a thorny situation."
b. "an easy and comfortable situation."
c. "a beautiful bed full of roses."
d. "a place where rose bushes are grown."

Appreciating Poetry

10. The writer of "Bears" uses his characters to criticize people who
   a. eat too much and get as big as bears.
   b. think that making rules about problems ends the problems.
   c. hunt bears.
   d. favor arbitration for the settlement of quarrels.

GROUP 3 Reread the poems in Group 3 to complete the following sentences.

Reviewing the Selection

11. The only thing that the pool players in "We Real Cool" do not brag about is
   a. dropping out of school.
   b. hanging out on the street most of the night.
   c. having good, reliable jobs.
   d. praising evil.

12. In "Sea Fever" the kind of vessel that the speaker wants to travel on is
   a. a modern whaling ship.
   b. a starship.
   c. a gypsy wagon.
   d. a sailing ship.

Recognizing How Words Are Used

13. Masefield probably called his poem "Sea Fever" because
   a. the speaker's desire to go to sea is upsetting him as much as an illness would.
   b. hot, feverish weather is making the speaker dream about going to sea.
   c. going to sea makes the speaker feel sick.
   d. the speaker is at sea and delirious with fever.

Interpreting the Selection

14. In "The Flower-Fed Buffaloes" the speaker
   a. is happy that the buffaloes are gone.
   b. feels bad because the buffaloes are gone.
   c. thinks it's funny that huge buffaloes would eat little flowers.
   d. is angry that the buffaloes ate all the flowers.

Appreciating Poetry

15. In "A Legend of Paul Bunyan" the moon is compared to
   a. a backpack.
   b. smoke from a pipe.
   c. a cloud.
   d. the headlight on a train.

Now check your answers with your teacher. Study the questions you answered incorrectly. What types of questions were they? Talk with your teacher about ways to work on those skills.

Sounds in Poetry

In choosing and arranging the words of a poem, a poet is alert to such matters as which sounds go together smoothly and which sounds force a reader to slow down. He or she also is concerned about which words or parts of words should be given more emphasis than others. Poets may even think about the shape the reader's mouth will take as it forms the sounds of words. Why are these matters important in poetry? Isn't the meaning of the words the only important thing?

To understand why sounds are as important as words are in poetry, consider why people are concerned about the colors of the clothes they wear. You know that certain colors look better on you than other colors. You know, also, that some colors make you feel better. You may even wear certain colors to celebrate an event—such as red, white, and blue for a patriotic holiday. You also may wear certain colors to associate yourself with a particular group—such as orange and blue for your favorite sports team.

Two jackets of different colors may be equally good at keeping you warm, but that doesn't mean they are equally fitting for a particular occasion. Similarly, two words may have almost identical definitions but may not be equally fitting for a particular line of poetry. Just as the colors of your clothes give meaning to what you wear, the sounds of words give meaning to what a poem says.

The lessons in this unit will discuss how poets use sounds to add "color" to a poem by focusing on the following techniques:

- Poets often arrange words to produce an easily noticeable rhythm.
- They may use rhyming words in regular patterns to reinforce that rhythm.

• Poets also may repeat particular consonant and vowel sounds to draw attention to certain words or to suggest certain sounds or moods.

LESSON 1 — LISTENING FOR RHYTHM

In poetry the term *rhythm* generally refers to the pattern of stressed and unstressed syllables. Listen, for example, to the word *information*. You hear four syllables, two *stressed* and two *unstressed*. The four syllables follow this pattern: stressed, unstressed, stressed, unstressed. You can show this pattern visually by drawing a slanted line (/) for each stressed syllable and a curved line (∪) for each unstressed syllable. These markings, then, represent the stresses, or beats, in *information*:

/　∪　/　∪

in　for　ma　tion

Compare the pattern you hear in *information* with the one you hear in *industrial*. These markings show the beats in *industrial*:

∪　/　∪　/

in　dus　tri　al

Which set of marks below stands for the pattern you hear in *wondering*?

/∪∪　　　　　　　　∪∪/

Even when you use only one-syllable words in a phrase, you put more stress on some words than on others. For example, you can hear the following pattern in the phrase *Once upon a time*:

/　∪/　∪　/

Once　upon　a　time

Some poems follow strict rhythms, or patterns of beats, from start to finish. Other poems, called *free verse*, sound more like conversation, with irregular rhythms throughout.

Still other poems use strong rhythmic patterns in selected lines for special effect.

"Annabel Lee" by Edgar Allan Poe is an example of the first type of poem, with a definite rhythmic pattern throughout. Read, for example, the first stanza:

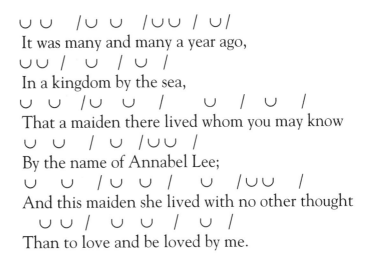

The first, third, and fifth lines have four stressed syllables, while the even-numbered lines have only three. Any two stressed syllables in the same line are separated by one or, usually, two unstressed syllables. We find it easy to get into this rhythm and are led forward almost irresistibly from one line to the next.

The fact that the rhythm is so regular produces a shock when it changes. Notice that in the fourth stanza there is a single phrase that uses two stressed syllables one after the other.

That the wind came out of the cloud chilling

And killing my Annabel Lee.

The stress on the first syllable of *chilling* is so unexpected that it makes that word jump out and demand attention, although the reader may not recognize why this happens.

Naming the rhythmic pattern of "Annabel Lee" is not important. What is important is what the rhythm does to make reading the poem a pleasant experience. It pulls readers into the story of the poem, carries them along with the musical flow, and then, by a small irregularity, startles them into a stronger awareness of the meaning. As you read poems in the future, listen for any rhythmic patterns and how they contribute to the meaning of each poem.

EXERCISE 1

Reread the poems in Group 1. Then use what you have learned in this lesson to answer the following questions:

1. The poem "Indians" is twelve lines long. Six of the lines follow the same rhythmic pattern. The other six follow no special pattern. Which are the lines that follow a pattern? Why do you suppose the poet used a strong rhythm in those particular lines? How does the difference between the two types of lines relate to the meaning of the poem?

2. Read the poem "Crossing" to hear the strong beats. If possible, find a partner and read the poem aloud. (You may need to read it more than once to get the rhythm just right.) Why do you think the writer changed the rhythm between the beginning and the end of the poem? How does the change in rhythm bring out the meaning of the poem?

Now check your answers with your teacher. Review this part of the lesson if you don't understand why an answer was incorrect.

WRITING ON YOUR OWN [1]

You have seen how poets use rhythm to establish a flowing sound, to focus attention, and to support meaning in poetry. Now you will have a turn choosing and arranging words to create a rhythm that brings out their meaning. Follow these steps:

- Imagine yourself walking with great energy down a long hall with no objects or people in your way. Write two sentences that describe how you are moving. Create a smooth, regular rhythm that suggests the speed and evenness of your progress, as in "I walk down the hall with my books in my arms, and I feel I could go on forever."
- Now imagine yourself walking on an uneven sidewalk, uphill, at the end of a long day. You are tired, and the walk is crowded with other people moving in both directions or cutting across from side to side. Write two sentences that describe how you are moving. Create a slow or irregular rhythm that is clearly different from the one you just created, as in "As I climb, slowly, up the hill, bikes, skateboards, and other pedestrians crowd, push, and get in my way."

LESSON 2 — LISTENING FOR RHYME AND RHYME PATTERNS

Two words are said to rhyme when their ending sounds match. In English we expect both the final vowel sound and any following consonant sounds to be the same in each of the rhyming words. For example, *shore* and *more* rhyme, but *short* and *more* do not. Two lines of poetry are said to rhyme when they end with words that rhyme. Here is an example of rhyming lines from "The Shark":

My dear, let me tell you about the shark.
Though his eyes are bright, his thought is dark.

Rhyme makes words easier to notice and remember. Because we don't often speak in rhyme, writing that uses rhyme automatically sets itself apart from normal conversation and grabs our attention.

Poets have traditionally taken advantage of the strengths of rhyme and have developed many patterns of rhyme, called *rhyme schemes*. They use single-syllable rhymes, such as *shark* and *dark*. They use two-syllable rhymes, such as the words *trying* and *flying* in "Wilbur Wright and Orville Wright." When they go so far as to use three-syllable rhymes, such as the words *perspicacity* and *loquacity* in "Bears," the rhyme almost covers up the meaning. Such rhyming patterns are usually reserved for a more light-hearted, comic effect.

Sometimes poets use words that almost rhyme. "The Shark," for instance, has this near-rhyme:

> With those two bright eyes and that one dark thought.
> He has only one but he thinks it a lot.

At other times, poets make up new words or think of new uses for words just to come up with words that rhyme. A good deal of the fun in "Wilbur Wright and Orville Wright" comes from the use of the brothers' initials in clever rhyming pairs such as *it is true*/W and *bro*/O.

Poets usually choose a particular pattern of rhythm, join it with a particular pattern of rhyme, and follow those patterns throughout the poem. When they change one pattern or the other, those different lines stand out. Notice what happens, for example, when the writer of "Crossing" changes the rhyme pattern in these lines:

> *Phoebe Snow, B&O,*
> **thirty-four, five,**
> *Santa Fe cattle*
> *shipped alive,*

> *red cars, yellow cars,*
> *orange cars, black,*
> *Youngstown steel*
> *down to Mobile*
> *on Rock Island track,*

The first four lines of this passage, like all the lines before it, have rhyming words at the end of every second line—*B&O, five, cattle, alive.* So we expect that the next four lines will follow the same pattern. Instead we see an extra rhyme and an extra line thrown in between *black* and its rhyme, *track—cars, black, steel, Mobile, track.* In this poem about the sound of a freight train, the extra, unexpected rhyme makes us think of a car jumping over some irregularity in the track.

There is a short and simple way of describing the rhyme scheme in a poem. Match a single letter with each end sound and reuse the letter when that end sound appears again. If the first two lines of a poem rhyme (*shark, dark*), write *aa.* If they have different end sounds (*Wright, trying*), write *ab.* In the first four lines quoted above, therefore (*B&O, five, cattle, alive*), the rhyme scheme is *abcb.* In the next five lines (*cars, black, steel, Mobile, track*), it is *deffe.*

For more information about the most popular combinations of patterns of rhyme and rhythm, see Unit 6.

EXERCISE 2

Reread the poems in Group 2. Then use what you have learned in this lesson to answer the following questions:

1. Examine all three poems for rhymes. In each poem identify a two-syllable rhyme.

2. "Bears" alternates between four-line stanzas and six-line stanzas. What is the rhyme scheme of each of these stanzas?

3. "Wilbur Wright and Orville Wright" alternates between sets of four lines that follow the *abcb* rhyme scheme and sets of four lines that follow a variation on that pattern. What is the second rhyme scheme you hear in this poem?

Now check your answers with your teacher. Review this part of the lesson if you don't understand why an answer was incorrect.

WRITING ON YOUR OWN ☐2

You have seen how some writers make use of rhyme to add interest and emphasis to their poems. Now it is your turn to write some rhyming poetry. Follow these steps:

- As a warm-up exercise choose at least one word-ending from each of the groups below and write it on a sheet of paper. Under the word-ending write all the words you can think of that have the same ending sound or sounds—but not necessarily the same spelling. For Group A the words may be one or more syllables long. For Group B they may be two or more syllables long. You should be able to come up with at least three rhymes for each.
  Group A   -ane   -eel   -irt   -ord   -un
  Group B   -atter   -illy   -ation
- Using rhyming words from your lists, write a four-line poem with either the *aabb* rhyme scheme or the *abcb* rhyme scheme. Try to use regular rhythms in your poem.

LESSON 3   LISTENING FOR OTHER SOUND TECHNIQUES

Rhythmic patterns and rhyming words are not the only sound techniques that poets use. They also can use other types of repetition and onomatopoeia. Following are the definitions of some of these techniques:

Repetition—the use of the same sounds, words, or phrases over and over. The use of repetition unifies a poem. It may also emphasize the rhythm, mood, or meaning of a passage or even suggest the sound of a thing being described.

Rhyme—the repetition of vowel and consonant sounds at the ends of words or lines.

Alliteration—the repetition of sounds in other parts of words, especially beginning consonants. An example of alliteration is the repetition of the /f/ sound in the title "The Flower-Fed Buffaloes." The /f/ sound occurs at the beginning of both *flower* and *fed* and in the middle of *buffaloes*.

Assonance—the repetition of vowel sounds in words. Hear, for example, the /oo/ sound in each of the first two words in this phrase from "The Flower-Fed Buffaloes": "bl<u>oo</u>ming, perf<u>u</u>med grass." The /i/ sound appears four times in this phrase: "<u>i</u>n the spr<u>i</u>ng that st<u>i</u>ll <u>i</u>s sweet."

A poet may choose to repeat a whole word or phrase to emphasize it. Notice how Vachel Lindsay stresses the coming of modern transportation by repeating *wheels* in the line "Wheels and wheels and wheels spin by." An additional effect of this repetition is the spinning sound it suggests.

Phrases repeated in the last third of the poem include "no more" and "lying low," each said three times. In addition, the phrase "lie low" appears near the beginning of the poem. By reusing a variation on this phrase at the end of the poem, Lindsay pulls the whole poem together.

Onomatopoeia—words that sound like what they mean. In these lines from "Wilbur Wright and Orville Wright," the sound that birds make is suggested by the onomatopoeia in "cheep-cheep":

> Said Orville Wright to Wilbur Wright,
> "These birds are very trying.
> I'm tired of hearing them cheep-cheep
> About the fun of flying.

Sometimes alliteration produces the effect of ono-matopoeia. For example, the /s/ and /z/ sounds can suggest the splashing of waves. See how John Masefield aimed for this effect in these lines of "Sea Fever":

> And the wheel's kick and the wind's song and the
>   white sail's shaking,
> And a gray mist on the sea's face and a gray dawn
>   breaking.

EXERCISE 3

Reread the poems in Group 3. Then use what you have learned in this lesson to answer the following questions.

1. In "We Real Cool" Brooks uses alliteration in almost every line.

    a. Which consonant sound is used four times in stanza 1? Identify the four other instances of alliteration in stanzas 2 through 4.

    b. In the second line of stanza 3, there is no alliteration, but another type of repetition links two words. What is that type of repetition?

    c. In the final line no consonant or vowel sounds are repeated. Why do you think the poet wrote these lines different from the rest?

2. Examine "Sea Fever" for examples of assonance and ono-matopoeia.

    a. In stanza 1, line 3, the long *a* sound occurs for the first time in the word *sail's*. How many times is this vowel sound repeated in the rest of that stanza? List the words in lines 3 and 4 in which you hear that vowel sound.

    b. The /w/ sound can suggest the sound of blowing, and therefore of wind. Identify the single line in stanzas 2 and 3 that uses /w/ the most times to suggest onomatopoeia.

3. In "A Legend of Paul Bunyan," the line lengths vary and the rhythm changes almost from line to line, so the technique used to hold this poem together is the repetition of sounds.

a.   Identify at least three examples of alliteration in lines 1 through 15.

b.   State whether each quotation below uses rhyme or assonance or both, and identify the matching sounds in different words:

Quote #1: swayed as he walked,
            as he talked

Quote #2: a huge, looming shadow
            of a man,
            clad
            in a mackinaw coat,

Quote #3: like thunder
            on a summer night

Quote #4: tangled,
            spangled
            in the branches of the great pine.

Now check your answers with your teacher. Review this part of the lesson if you don't understand why an answer was incorrect.

 WRITING ON YOUR OWN ⟨3⟩

In this exercise you will practice using alliteration and assonance to link words or give them emphasis. Follow these steps:

• Repetition of sounds is often used in advertising copy to make products more memorable, as in "delightful dancing dolls." Imagine you are writing advertisements to sell three items located around the room. First choose the three items. Then write a sentence describing each item. Use alliteration in at least four words in each sentence.

- Choose one of the ads for further development. Write a second sentence about the item for sale, explaining what it can used for. Use the same vowel sound in at least three words in your second sentence.
- Write a third sentence about the object using onomatopoeia. For example, you might describe how the object works or sounds.
- Write a fourth sentence that pulls the whole ad together with the use of repetition, either of parts of words or of whole words or phrases. The repetition in the fourth sentence should create links with the earlier sentences.

DISCUSSION GUIDES

1. Which of the poems in this unit would you choose to share with a person of your grandparents' generation? Be able to explain your reasons for choosing those poems. Join a group of classmates and compare your choices. Are there any poems that show up on several students' lists? Why or why not? As soon as possible, read the poems you chose to the older person you had in mind. Report back to your group how the person reacted to the poems.

2. Several of the poems in Unit 4 concern people or events in American history. List those poems. Did reading any of them give you a new attitude or understanding of the people or events being described? Did any of the poems make you want to learn more about the people or events? Discuss how the poem or poems affected your thinking, and why.

3. Alone or with a small group, choose a poem from this unit to present before your classmates. Take a day to practice reading the poem with expression. If it is short, try to memorize it. Then perform the poem for your whole class or a smaller group of students.

4. With a partner rearrange the poems in this unit according to a grouping of your choice—by topic, speaker, mood, date of composition, or whatever you like. You may drop up to three of the poems that don't fit your organization. Make out a table of contents for your poems, listing them in the order you choose. Use subtitles or notes that explain why the poems are in that particular order. Post or exchange your table of contents with those of other students and compare your ways of grouping the poems.

WRITE A POEM ABOUT AN EVENT

In this unit you have examined how the sounds in poems give them shape and unity and support their meaning. In the writing exercises you have practiced using many sound techniques. Now you will use what you have learned to write an original poem that makes use of rhythm, rhyme, and repetition.

Follow these steps to write your poem. If you have questions about the writing process, refer to Using the Writing Process on page 235.

- Assemble the work you did for all the writing exercises in this unit: 1) three lists of possible topics for writing, 2) two prose descriptions of walking under different circumstances, 3) a short poem using a definite rhyme scheme, 4) advertising copy about an object.

- Review your lists of possible topics as well as the topics of the poems in this unit. In the course of reading and discussing the poems, you may have developed more ideas for topics you want to write about. List those too. Now choose a topic that involves a single event, such as the passing of a freight train in "Crossing" or Paul Bunyan's walk across the valley in "A Legend of Paul Bunyan." Your event may be real or imagined.

- Choose how many stressed syllables you will have in each line. For example, will the line usually stress only one syllable of any two, as in "Now the nurse will test your sight"? Or will it have two unstressed syllables between stressed ones, as in "This is a test of your sight"? You may want to write a few lines of your poem before you make your decision, to see which pattern comes naturally.

- Decide which rhyme scheme you intend to use—*aabb, abcb,* or something else. With your topic or event in mind, write several words that you are likely to use in describing it. Then brainstorm for as many rhymes as you can think of for each of those words. Even if you don't use any of the words on your list, thinking of rhyming words will help you practice. Don't forget about two-syllable or longer rhymes.
- Now write your poem. In the poem tell who or what is involved, where and when the event takes place, how the event occurred and ended, and any lasting result or lesson from the event. As you write, keep in mind the sound devices you have studied and use them wherever possible. If you must revise either your rhyme scheme or rhythm, do so as you write. Write as many stanzas as you need, but try to keep your poem to fewer than 24 lines long.
- Reread your poem aloud to a classmate and have him or her answer these questions: Is the description of the event easy to understand and picture? Is the rhythm fairly regular? Is the rhyme scheme clear? Did the poem use alliteration and assonance at least a few times each? Was there onomatopoeia? Make any changes that you feel are necessary.
- Proofread your poem for spelling and grammar errors. When you are finished, make a final copy of your poem and save it in your writing portfolio.

Figurative Language

INTRODUCTION

ABOUT THE LESSONS

As you have learned, some poems try to capture particular scenes or experiences in words. They focus on what can be seen, heard, or otherwise sensed at a particular moment and in a particular place. Other poems make objects or experiences more meaningful by comparing one thing with another thing that seems quite different. As you discover what the two things have in common, you'll probably notice certain qualities of both things that you've never seen before. A poet can use *figurative language* to bring together and compare unexpected things. Figurative language includes the use of *figures of speech* and *imagery*. In this unit you will examine different kinds of figurative language and will discover how each kind helps express the meaning of a poem.

WRITING: USING FIGURATIVE LANGUAGE

Throughout this unit you will learn about different kinds of figurative language and their effects on a poem. At the end of the unit you will write a poem that makes use of some of these figures of speech. Begin warming up by following these steps:

• Keep a record of odd combinations used in TV, radio, and print advertisements that make people think about a product in a particular way. For example, a soft drink ad might show polar bears or penguins with the drink to suggest how cold and refreshing it is, or it might show fireworks exploding from the container to suggest that its taste is exciting. If the ad states a comparison, such as "tastes as smooth and cool as ice," record that comparison. Otherwise, note the image that the ad matches up with the product and the idea or feeling that you think the advertiser intends to express.

- *Cliches* are overused phrases, such as the comparisons "sharp as a tack," "fresh as a daisy," or "pretty as a picture." Start a list of clichés that you find in advertisements, news programs and news articles, and other places, so that you can avoid using them. If you are not sure whether a particular phrase is a cliché, add it to your list and ask classmates whether have come across the same comparison.
- After adding entries to both of these lists for three or four days, meet with a partner or small group to compare what you have found. Choose the two or three most effective combinations among the ads. Choose the two or three clichés that seem the least meaningful to you.
- Save your lists to use later in the unit.

ABOUT THIS POET

Eve Merriam (1916–1992) was an award-winning poet, playwright, and biographer who tried to encourage a love of poetry in others, particularly children. She also was deeply interested in such social issues as sexual equality, racial justice, war, the environment, and technology. Since these issues affect children's lives, she discussed them in her poems for children as well as in her writing for adults.

Merriam was born in Philadelphia, Pennsylvania, into a book-loving family. She was fascinated by words and poetry at an early age and began writing her own poems by the time she was eight years old. After graduating from the University of Pennsylvania in 1937, she began graduate studies at Columbia University in New York City. However, she soon left school to become an advertising copywriter; then a radio writer, columnist, and fashion editor; and finally a freelance writer of poetry, fiction, nonfiction, and plays.

Merriam won a poetry prize for *Family Circle* (1946), the first of her eight poetry books for adults. She published her first book of poetry for children, *There Is No Rhyme for*

Silver, in 1962. She produced 16 more volumes of poetry for children in the following 30 years. In *Finding a Poem* (1970), Merriam included a report of how she wrote one of the selections, a poem that went through 12 revisions! She won the National Council of Teachers of English Award for Excellence in Children's Poetry in 1981. Merriam has been described as "a most influential voice in educating teachers of children's literature."

AS YOU READ

As you read each poem in this unit, ask yourself these questions about figurative language:

- In what unusual ways does this poet use figurative language? What unusual comparisons does he or she make? Why?
- How does the poet's unusual use of language help express the theme of this poem? Could the same idea be expressed equally well in other words?

Primer Lesson

by Carl Sandburg

ABOUT THE SELECTION

Carl Sandburg (1878–1967) is one of the most important modern poets in the United States. He was born in Galesburg, Illinois, and left school at the age of 13 for a series of jobs in the West. After returning to Illinois to attend Lombard College, he became a journalist in Chicago. When his first book of poetry was published in 1916, he became nationally known as a writer for both adults and children. Sandburg won two Pulitzer Prizes: one for his poetry and the second for his six-volume biography of Abraham Lincoln. Much of his writing praised folk wisdom and the common man. His poem "Primer Lesson" (which means first, or beginning, lesson) advises us to think before we speak because once words are spoken, they cannot be taken back.

Look out how you use proud words.
When you let proud words go, it is
   not easy to call them back.
They wear long boots, hard boots; they
   walk off proud; they can't hear
   you calling—
Look out how you use proud words.

Like Bookends

by Eve Merriam

ABOUT THE SELECTION

Eve Merriam (1916–1992) received a number of awards for her poetry, plays, and fiction. She wrote more than 30 books, many of them for young readers. Her poetry often focuses on social issues, such as women's rights. "Like Bookends" takes a look at family life from an odd angle. For more information about Merriam, see About This Poet at the beginning of this unit.

Like bookends
my father at one side
my mother at the other

propping me up
but unable to read
what I feel.

Were they born with clothes on?
Born with rules on?

When we sit at the dinner table
we smooth our napkins into polite folds.
How was your day dear
          Fine
 And how was yours dear
          Fine
And how was school
          The same

Only once in a while
when we're not trying so hard
when we're not trying at all
our napkins suddenly whirl away
and we float up to the ceiling
where we sing and dance until it hurts from laughing

and then we float down
with our napkin parachutes
and once again spoon our soup
and pass the bread please.

Words

by Pauli Murray

ABOUT THE SELECTION

Besides being a poet, Pauli Murray (1910–1985) was also a civil rights activist, an attorney, and a clergywoman. Although born in Baltimore, Maryland, Murray spent many years in North Carolina. Orange County, North Carolina, honors her community work by presenting an annual Pauli Murray Human Relations Youth Award. Murray became an attorney in 1945, and in 1977 she was ordained an Episcopal priest. She also took part in the founding of NOW (the National Organization for Women). Many of her poems appeared in magazines and anthologies, as well as in her book *The Dark Testament and Other Poems.* The poem you are about to read, "Words," focuses on a subject important in all of her careers.

We are spendthrifts with words,
We squander[1] them,
Toss them like pennies in the air—
Arrogant[2] words,
Angry words,
Cruel words,
Comradely[3] words,
Shy words tiptoeing from mouth to ear.

---

[1] waste

[2] full of pride and self-importance

[3] friendly

But the slowly wrought words of love
And the thunderous words of heartbreak—
These we hoard.[4]

---

[4] collect and hide

sun

by Valerie Worth

ABOUT THE SELECTION

Valerie Worth (1933–1994) was born in Philadelphia and graduated from Swarthmore College. Among Worth's books are a series on "small" poems—from *Small Poems* (1972) through *More Small Poems* (1976) to *All the Small Poems and Fourteen More* (1994). In 1991 Worth won the National Council of Teachers of English Award for Excellence in Poetry. This poem reflects her belief that poetry should be about "that which changes slowly."

The sun
Is a leaping fire
Too hot
To go near,

But it will still
Lie down
In warm yellow squares
On the floor

Like a flat
Quilt, where
The cat can curl
And purr.

Cumulus Clouds

by Sheryl L. Nelms

ABOUT THE SELECTION

Many of the poems that Sheryl L. Nelms writes are being printed in small poetry magazines, including some that are published on the Internet. Nelms also writes young-adult fiction. In "Cumulus Clouds," she suggests a fresh, unique approach to a familiar scene.

a gallon of
rich
country cream

hand-whipped
into stiff
peaks

flung
from the beater

into dollops[1]
across the blue oilcloth[2]

---

[1] soft masses, lumps, or blobs

[2] cloth that is made waterproof by oil or coats of paint, often used to cover tables

In the Waiting Room

by Charles Reznikoff

ABOUT THE SELECTION

After taking a year of college journalism classes, Charles Reznikoff (1894–1976) decided to be a writer. His parents insisted that he finish college, however, so he entered New York University's law school because he thought he could combine writing with law. He graduated in 1915 and began practicing law, but soon went into sales and then editing so he could find time for writing. Whenever he had a collection of poems ready, Reznikoff published them privately. Still, he was never content with his work and often revised poems when he reprinted them. His first commercially published book appeared in 1962. After that, all the poems he had previously printed were published commercially. "In the Waiting Room" is an example of Reznikoff's fine attention to detail.

The Chinese girl in the waiting-room of the busy railway
station
writing on a pad
in columns
as if she were adding figures
instead of words—
words in blue ink
that look like small flowers
stylized[1] into squares:
she is planting a small private garden.

———
[1] designed according to a certain style or pattern

Song for a Surf-Rider

Sara Van Alstyne Allen

ABOUT THE SELECTION

In "Song for a Surf-Rider," poet Sara Van Alstyne Allen uses some very striking and unusual figurative language when she compares the sea to a horse—and surfing to horseback riding.

I ride the horse that is the sea.
His mane of foam flows wild and free.
His eyes flash with an emerald[1] fire.
His mighty heart will never tire.
His hoofbeats echo on the sand.
He quivers[2] as I raise my hand.
We race together, the sea and I,
Under the watching summer sky
To where the magic islands lie.

---

[1]a bright-green, transparent precious stone; the color of this stone

[2]trembles; shakes

Whirlwind Is a Ghost Dancing

a Dakota Poem retold by Natalia Belting

ABOUT THE SELECTION

Natalia Belting (1915–   ) taught history at the University of Illinois for several years and has written numerous books on history and folklore. She has taken particular interest in translating the folk literature of Native Americans into modern English.

The Dakota Sioux, part of the Sioux people, originally lived in Minnesota. Around 1860 they were driven westward by white settlement, but they battled for 30 years before being forced onto reservations. Now about half of all Sioux live on reservations in the northern plains; the rest are scattered in big cities across the United States. "Whirlwind Is a Ghost Dancing" gives a brief glimpse of life on the plains.

Wind is a ghost
That whirls and turns,
Twists in fleet moccasins,
Sweeps up dust spinning
Across the dry flatlands.

Whirlwind
Is a ghost dancing.

Sunset

by Oswald Mbuyiseni Mtshali

ABOUT THE SELECTION

Oswald Mbuyiseni Mtshali (1940–   ) was born in South Africa and began his writing career under that country's system of *apartheid* (racial segregation). For a time he was held under house arrest because of his opposition to apartheid. Today he is considered one of his country's major writers and is known as one of South Africa's "poets of the big cities." His books of poetry include *Sounds of a Cowhide Drum* (1972) and *Fireflames* (1980). In "Sunset" Mtshali combines a scene in nature with modern city life.

The sun spun like
a tossed coin.
It whirled on the azure[1] sky,
it clattered into the horizon,
it clicked in the slot,
and neon-lights popped
and blinked "Time expired,"
as on a parking meter.

---

[1] a clear, bright blue color

UNDERSTANDING THE POEMS
Record your answers to these questions in your personal literature notebook. Follow the directions for each group.

GROUP 1   Reread the poems in Group 1 to complete these sentences.

Reviewing the
Selection

1. In the poem "sun" the sun is compared to
   a. a fire and a floor.
   b. a fire and a quilt.
   c. a fire and a cat.
   d. a quilt and a cat.

Interpreting the
Selection

2. In "Words" the kind of words that "tiptoe from mouth to ear" are probably words that often
   a. are whispered in secret.
   b. are told to a make a person laugh.
   c. tickle a person's ear.
   d. take a long time to get to a person's ear.

3. In "Primer Lesson," *proud words* are considered
   a. words that make you feel good.
   b. words that mean the same thing as *proud*.
   c. elegant, unusual words that are difficult to understand.
   d. words meant to make someone else feel small.

Recognizing How
Words Are Used

4. In "Cumulus Clouds" two words that suggest energy and movement are *hand-whipped* and
   a. *stiff.*
   b. *peaks.*
   c. *flung.*
   d. *oilcloth.*

Appreciating Poetry

5. In "Like Bookends" the speaker's attitude toward his or her parents is one of
  a. puzzlement.
  b. anger.
  c. total delight.
  d. great disappointment.

GROUP 2   Reread the poems in Group 2 to complete these sentences.

Reviewing the Selection

6. A hint that "Whirlwind Is a Ghost Dancing" is a Native-American poem is the use of the word
  a. *ghost.*
  b. *moccasins.*
  c. *flatland.*
  d. *whirlwind.*

7. The girl described in "In the Waiting-Room" is
  a. writing on a pad of paper.
  b. adding figures.
  c. drawing flowers.
  d. drawing plans for a garden.

Interpreting the Selection

8. The most important thought of "Sunset" is that
  a. both the sun and coins are round.
  b. parking meters require coins.
  c. many sunsets are beautiful.
  d. every person's time is limited.

Recognizing How Words Are Used

9. In "Song for a Surf-Rider," the poet uses the phrase *emerald fire* instead of *green fire* because
  a. *emerald* is a fancier word, and she wants to impress her readers.
  b. fire isn't really green.
  c. she is comparing the horse's eyes to the gems called emeralds.
  d. the horse's eyes flash green fire when it looks at things.

Appreciating Poetry   **10.** Of the following, the most striking characteristic of "Sunset" is its
   a. intricate rhyme scheme.
   b. strong, expressive verbs.
   c. details that appeal to all five senses.
   d. mood of awe at the beauty of nature.

Now check your answers with your teacher. Study the questions you answered incorrectly. What types of questions were they? Talk with your teacher about ways to work on those skills.

Figurative Language

Imagine a shoe box in which a child has stored a collection of marbles and small balls, keys and coins, and other small objects. Analyze your feelings about that box. Very likely, you have no particular emotion for or against it. Suppose, however, that the box were called a treasure chest. Your reaction probably would change. You automatically would feel more positive and excited about the shoe box. On the other hand, if the box were described as a miniature land-fill, your reaction toward it would be negative. Why would your reactions change from neutral to positive or negative? There was nothing different about the box and its contents. However, there was something different about the way you looked at the box—and that difference was caused by the connections you made between the box and other things in your experience.

Poets know about the power of making connections and altering your view of a thing. They use language in special ways to take advantage of that power. The special effects they create include metaphors, similes, and other expressions known as *figures of speech*, or *figurative language*. This unit will discuss the following uses of figurative language:

- Metaphors, similes, and other figures of speech help poets lead readers to look at common objects in uncommon ways.
- Metaphors, similes, and other figures of speech affect the meaning and impact of a poem.

LESSON 1 | FIGURES OF SPEECH

Metaphors, similes, and personification are all figures of speech that make comparisons between two unlike objects. In each comparison, a writer asks readers to recognize a way in which the two things are alike. The writer also may expect readers to transfer their feelings about one object to the other object.

A metaphor compares two unlike things by saying that one is the other. Look, for example, at these lines from the poem "Like Bookends."

> and then we float down
> with our napkin parachutes

The table napkins are not simply napkins; they have become parachutes. For a few minutes they have lost their "polite folds" and have acquired an excitement that demonstrates the special quality of the moment that the poem describes. A metaphor that is developed over several lines or stanzas of a poem is called an *extended metaphor*.

The poem "Words" begins with another type of metaphor. *Spendthrifts* are people who use money foolishly, but the poem says "we are spendthrifts with words." The poet does not say that words are money, but her words imply that idea. This type of metaphor is an *implied metaphor*.

A *simile* is a comparison between unlike things that uses such words as *like* or *as*. Line 1 of "Words" has an implied metaphor that words are money, but line 3 has a simile that gets more specific:

> We are spendthrifts with words,
> We squander them,
> Toss them like pennies in the air—

This simile compares words with pennies, our least valuable coins, to show how carelessly we use them and how little attention we give them.

Personification is a figure of speech that gives human characteristics to objects, ideas, and other nonhuman things. Notice how both "Words" and "Primer Lesson" personify words. In each case the poem begins by relating the attitude of the person saying the words with the words themselves. Example 1 below lists several attitudes towards words, while Example 2 focuses on just one:

Example 1
Arrogant words,
Angry words,
Cruel words,
Comradely words,

Example 2
Look out how you use proud words.

Then each poem describes words behaving as if they were the people who said them:

Example 1
Shy words tiptoeing from mouth to ear.

Example 2
When you let proud words go, it is
        not easy to call them back.
They wear long boots, hard boots; they
        walk off proud; they can't hear
        you calling—

Prose writers also use metaphors, similes, and personification, but much less frequently than poets do. If you watch for these figures of speech as you read, you will find at least one of them in almost every poem.

EXERCISE 1

Reread the poems in Group 1. Then use what you have learned in this lesson to answer the following questions:

1. To what is the sun being compared in the poem "sun"? What figure of speech is each comparison? How are the objects like the sun in each comparison?

2. Which figure of speech—metaphor, simile, or personification—do you find in "Cumulus Clouds"? What two things are being compared? In what way are they alike?

Now check your answers with your teacher. Review this part of the lesson if you don't understand why an answer was incorrect.

 WRITING ON YOUR OWN 1

In this exercise you will practice writing some figures of speech. Follow these steps:

- The poems in Group 1 used figures of speech to describe time, words, and things found in nature. Choose something that you might use every day, such as a pencil, a bus, or a refrigerator. In what way is this object important or useful to you? Is there another, unlike thing that is known for the same characteristic? How could you compare these two objects in order to suggest your feelings about your chosen object? For example, you may dislike the bus because it is noisy and drafty. How could you emphasize the noise and the cold winds that blow through the vehicle? Could you compare the bus to an old-fashioned airplane with no cabin or an open sleigh drawn by noisy reindeer? Maybe you like the bus because you meet friends on it. Could you compare it to a party on wheels? List several objects with which you could compare your chosen item.
- Select an object on your comparison list and write a metaphor that indicates how your chosen item is like that object. For example, if you decide to compare the bus with

an antique airplane, you might write, "The bus I ride is a low-flying biplane with an open cockpit, where there is no protection from the wind."

- Choose another of the objects on your list and write a simile that shows how your chosen item is like that object. For example, here is a simile comparing the bus to a party: "The bus I ride is like a rolling party, where we talk and play games every day."
- Find some aspect of the situation you have been describing that can be pictured as a human. Write a statement that personifies that aspect. For example, you might write, "Every time I get on the bus, the wind comes aboard too. It sits down in front of me, turns around in its seat, and whispers cold words to me."

LESSON 2 | **HOW FIGURATIVE LANGUAGE EXPRESSES THEME**

When poet Pauli Murray says that our words are like pennies tossed in the air, she is implying that we don't value words. This simile also reminds us that even pennies are worth something and that we are foolish not to remember that words have value too. That's quite a bit of meaning for just a few words. But that is typical of figurative language. It squeezes a great deal of meaning into a single statement or phrase. In many poems a single strong figure of speech expresses the *theme*, or message, of the entire poem.

Recall the poem "In the Waiting Room." The first eight lines simply describe a scene in the waiting room of a busy train station. The poet tells how a Chinese girl is writing in columns rather than from side to side, as in the Western writing system. He points out that the Chinese symbols look like square flowers. The ninth line summarizes the girl's writing in a metaphor: "she is planting a small private garden."

Suddenly the writing symbols do not simply *look* like flowers; they *are* flowers. Further, they are flowers in a garden that is private despite the fact that the girl is in the middle of a busy station. We understand that the girl's writing has separated her from her surroundings and taken her into a world of her own. Through this metaphor the poet expresses the theme that writing—especially in a language that most others can't read—can take us beyond our immediate setting.

In any figure of speech the poet connects two unlike things and explains or suggests why he or she links them. Two different poems may make similar comparisons for very different purposes. Look, for example, at "Words" and "Sunset." In each poem the poet compares something in nature to money. In "Words" words are compared to pennies and are spent or hoarded like money. In "Sunset" the sun is described as spinning like "a tossed coin." However, the poems use these comparisons to money to express very different themes.

"Words" points out the power of language and its effect on our emotions. The poet admonishes the reader to think before speaking—to be as careful about using words as he or she might be about using money.

In "Sunset" we are made aware of constant action. The sun *spun, whirled, clattered,* and *clicked* in the slot, meaning it dropped below the horizon. The metaphor of the sun as a coin in action suggests a hurried, harried mood. The metaphor goes on to a surprising conclusion that expresses the theme that time passes too quickly:

> it clicked in the slot,
> and neon-lights popped
> and blinked "Time expired,"
> as on a parking meter.

Clearly, it is not enough to notice only which two unlike things are being compared in a metaphor, simile, or other figure of speech. You must also determine in what way the poet connects the two things. That connection may state in just a few words the entire message of the poem.

EXERCISE 2

Reread the poems in Group 2. Then use what you
have learned in this lesson to answer the following
questions:

1. Find the extended metaphor in "Song for a Surf-Rider."
   What things does the metaphor compare? Do the details
   in the metaphor focus on how the things look, what they
   are used for, how they move, or some other characteristic?
   What is the theme that the metaphor and its details
   express?

2. Reread "Whirlwind Is a Ghost Dancing" and then answer
   the same questions for this poem that you answered for
   "Song for a Surf-Rider."

 WRITING ON YOUR OWN 2

In this exercise you will use figurative language to express
two opposing themes. Follow these steps:

- Choose an article of clothing and think of it in a positive
  way. For example, you might choose a jacket and imagine
  it to be warm, stylish, comfortable, and made of expensive
  fabric. Write a metaphor or simile that compares your article of clothing—or you wearing that article of clothing—to
  an animal of your choice. Your metaphor or simile should
  express a positive characteristic of the clothing or your attitude when you wear it.
- Next, imagine a negative example of the same type of
  clothing. For example, the second jacket you might imagine is dirty, frayed, cheaply made, and ill-fitting. Write a
  second metaphor or simile that compares the clothing, or
  you wearing it, to a different animal. This figure of speech
  must express a negative characteristic of the clothing or
  your attitude when wearing it.

DISCUSSION GUIDES

1. Several poems in this unit discuss the importance of words in various situations. Do you agree that people do not give enough thought to spoken words? Do you think it is possible to think about words as much before speaking them as before writing them? Why or why not? With a small group come up with several guidelines for avoiding doing damage with spoken words.

2. If you were creating an anthology of poems, which poems from this unit would you choose to include? How would you group your choices? Why? List the poems that you would use in the order you would use them. Then choose any poems from other units you have read in this book and add them to your list. Briefly explain the reasons for your choices.

3. Review the biographical notes that are supplied with some of the poems in this unit. Discuss the following questions with a group of classmates and then briefly report on your conclusions:
   - Could the poet's ideas and words have been influenced by his or her education, occupation, or hobbies?
   - Could the poet's education, occupation, or hobbies have influenced his or her ideas and words?

4. Choose a poem from this unit to present to your classmates. Memorize it and practice presenting it with expression. Then perform the poem for your class.

WRITE A POEM CONTAINING FIGURATIVE LANGUAGE

In this unit you have examined different figures of speech and their functions in poems. Now you will use what you have learned to write a poem that uses one or more figures of speech to express its theme.

Follow these steps to write your poem. If you have questions about the writing process, refer to Using the Writing Process on page 235.

- Assemble and review the work you did for all the writing exercises in this unit: 1) lists of effective and ineffective comparisons from advertising and other sources; 2) original figures of speech, in prose, about an object or experience in your own life; 3) two figures of speech involving clothing and animals.
- Review your original metaphors, similes, and statements that personify things. Select one of them to work with, or develop a new figure of speech involving an object or experience from your daily life.
- You can decide whether to use free verse or rhyme and rhythm in your poem. However, be sure to use alliteration, assonance, or both, to add interest to your words.
- Write a poem that includes your chosen figure of speech. Try to keep it to 12 lines or less. Make sure your readers will be able to understand the comparison you are making and why you are making it.
- Ask a classmate to read your poem aloud. Invite his or her reaction to both the figure of speech and how well it expresses your meaning. If necessary, revise your poem and have your classmate read it again.
- When you have finished any necessary revisions, proofread your poem for spelling and grammar errors. Then make a final copy of it and save it in your writing portfolio.

Form in Poetry

INTRODUCTION

ABOUT THE LESSONS

The term *form* is defined as the shape or outline of a thing or as the arrangement of its parts. In poetry *form* can refer to the patterns of sound in a spoken poem, the organization of its lines and stanzas, its appearance in writing, or all of these characteristics. In this unit you will look at the role of form in poetry. The poems in Group 1 illustrate a variety of forms defined by patterns of rhyme and rhythm. The poems in Group 2 include examples of special forms of poetry.

WRITING: USING FORM IN A POEM

In this unit you will learn about specific poetic forms and will be given opportunities to write in those forms. In this exercise you can begin thinking about topics that you might write about. Follow these steps:

- Do you keep a journal? If you don't, begin one now. Keep a small notepad handy. Several times a day, whenever you see or experience something interesting, jot down some notes about it. Your notes can be about people or scenes, feelings you have, things that have happened, questions you wonder about, or anything else you might want to recall later or share with others. Your journal can become a source of ideas when you want to write poetry or other kinds of writing.

- In your journal, list all the writing formats you can think of in which words, phrases, and sentences are communicated. Include traditional forms, such as friendly letters and magazine or newspaper articles. Include odd forms of print material, such as fortunes in fortune cookies and information on packaging. List electronic forms of communication, such as neon signs and the "crawl" that crosses the bottom of the television screen to warn viewers of a coming storm. Note special characteristics of each entry on your list, such as whether the words are arranged in single columns, multiple columns, or no columns at all; whether the positions of the words or the words themselves change over time; and so on.

ABOUT THIS POET

Myra Cohn Livingston (1926–1996) was a poet, an anthologist, and an educator. When she began writing poetry, she wrote for her children about her own happy childhood. As she worked with children to help them learn about poetry, however, she began to realize that many children have to deal with major problems, such as poverty or unstable home lives. The topics of her writing broadened to include such issues as race relations, the environment, loneliness, and death. Her poetry was noted for its uncomplicated style and its ability to capture a mood or a glimpse of natural beauty.

Born in Omaha, Nebraska, Livingston became a talented musician. While she was in high school, she began playing the French horn professionally. By the time she graduated from Sarah Lawrence College in 1948, however, she had decided to concentrate on writing. She worked as a book reviewer for newspapers and as a secretary until her marriage in 1952. Her first book of poetry for children, *Whispers and Other Poems*, published in 1958, won an award from the *New York Herald Tribune* Children's Spring Book Festival.

Over the next 40 years Livingston published several dozen more books of her own poetry and a number of highly praised anthologies of children's poems. She won numerous awards, including the 1980 National Council of Teachers of English Award for Excellence in Poetry.

During most of her career, Livingston combined her own writing with teaching creative writing, first to children and later to adults. Yet she once wrote, "No one can teach creative writing. . . . One can only make children aware of their sensitivities, and help children learn of the forms, the basic tools of poetry, into which they can put their own voices." And in an interview, she said that "Form makes you work harder to say important things. . . . Form doesn't permit you to go babbling off to no account. . . . The poetic soul or spirit is born. But the craft must be learned so that what is felt can then be expressed."

AS YOU READ

As you read the poems in this unit, ask yourself these questions about form:

- What forms do these poems take? Are there any forms, or patterns, of poems that are more common than others? How do I recognize and describe them?
- Are there forms of poems that have more rules than others? What sorts of rules do they follow?

When I Heard the Learn'd Astronomer

by Walt Whitman

ABOUT THE SELECTION

Walt Whitman (1819–1892) is still considered one of America's greatest poets. The publication of his book *Leaves of Grass* (1855) is considered a major event in the history of poetry because of its unusual style and forceful language. Many of Whitman's poems praise the United States and its system of democracy, which he thought would improve the human race. Whitman was born on Long Island, New York, grew up in Brooklyn, and later worked as a schoolteacher, a printer, and a journalist. During the Civil War he was a government clerk and volunteered at military hospitals. He had to resign from his government work in 1873 after having a stroke, but he continued to write for many years.

When I heard the learn'd astronomer,
When the proofs, the figures, were ranged in columns
    before me,
When I was shown the charts and diagrams, to add, divide,
    and measure them,
When I sitting heard the astronomer where he lectured
    with much applause in the lecture-room,
How soon unaccountable[1] I became tired and sick,
Till rising and gliding out I wander'd off by myself,
In the mystical[2] moist night-air, and from time to time,
Look'd up in perfect silence at the stars.

---

[1] unable to be explained

[2] spiritually significant; mysterious; beyond human understanding

The Skater of Ghost Lake

by William Rose Benét

ABOUT THE SELECTION

William Rose Benét (1886–1950) won the Pulitzer Prize for poetry in 1942 for his autobiographical narrative poem *The Dust Which Was God.* Besides being a poet, Benét was a critic and an editor who helped found *The Saturday Review of Literature* in 1924. He also served as the first editor of *The Reader's Encyclopedia* in 1948. Benét was married to another famous poet, Elinor Wylie. Like his younger brother, poet Stephen Vincent Benét (see Unit 4), William Rose Benét drew some of his material from American folklore. "The Skater of Ghost Lake" is a narrative poem, as are many of his works.

Ghost Lake's a dark lake, a deep lake and cold:
Ice black as ebony, frostily scrolled;[1]
Far in its shadows a faint sound whirrs;[2]
Steep stand the sentineled deep, dark firs.

A brisk sound, a swift sound, a ring-tinkle-ring;
Flit-flit—a shadow, with a stoop and a swing,
Flies from a shadow through the crackling cold.
Ghost Lake's a deep lake, a dark lake and old!

---

[1] decorated with spiral or coiled forms

[2] create a whizzing or buzzing sound, as by the motion of a bird's wings

Leaning and leaning, with a stride and a stride,
Hands locked behind him, scarf blowing wide,
Jeremy Randall skates, skates late,
Star for a candle, moon for a mate.

Black is the clear glass now that he glides,
Crisp is the whisper of long lean strides,
Swift is his swaying—but pricked ears hark.
None comes to Ghost Lake late after dark!

Cecily only—yes, it is she!
Stealing to Ghost Lake, tree after tree,
Kneeling in snow by the still lake side,
Rising with feet winged, gleaming, to glide.

Dust of the ice swirls. Here is his hand.
Brilliant his eyes burn. Now, as was planned,
Arm across arm twined,[3] laced to his side,
Out on the dark lake lightly they glide.

Dance of the dim moon, a rhythmical reel,
A swaying, a swift tune—skurr[4] of the steel;
Moon for a candle, maid for a mate,
Jeremy Randall skates, skates late.

Black as if lacquered[5] the wide lake lies;
Breath is a frost-fume, eyes seek eyes;
Souls are a sword-edge tasting the cold.
Ghost Lake's a deep lake, a dark lake and old!

----

[3] twisted together; tangled

[4] the same as *skirr*, an echoic word meaning *whir* or *whirr*

[5] coated with lacquer, a glossy liquid obtained originally from trees

Far in the shadows hear faintly begin
Like a string pluck-plucked of a violin,
Muffled in mist on the lake's far bound,
Swifter and swifter, a low singing sound!

Far in the shadows and faint on the verge
Of blue cloudy moonlight, see it emerge,
Flit-flit—a phantom,[6] with a stoop and a
    swing . . .
Ah, it's a night bird, burdened of wing!

Pressed close to Jeremy, laced to his side,
Cecily Culver, dizzy you glide.
Jeremy Randall sweepingly veers
Out on the dark ice far from the piers.[7]

"Jeremy!" "Sweetheart?" "What do you fear?"
"Nothing, my darling—nothing is here!"
"Jeremy?" "Sweetheart?" "What do you flee?"
"Something—I know not; something I see!"

Swayed to a swift stride, brisker of pace,
Leaning and leaning, they race and they race;
Ever that whirring, that crisp sound thin
Like a string pluck-plucked of a violin;

Ever that swifter and low singing sound
Sweeping behind them, winding them round;
Gasp of their breath now that chill flakes fret:
Ice black as ebony—blacker—like jet!

---

[6] someone or something that seems to be sensed but has no physical reality

[7] platform extending from a shore over water and supported by pillars

Ice shooting fangs forth—sudden like spears;
Crackling of lightning—a roar in their ears!
Shadowy, a phantom swerves off from its
    prey . . .
No, it's a night bird flit-flits away!

Low-winging moth-owl, home to your sleep!
Ghost Lake's a still lake, a cold lake and deep.
Faint in its shadows a far sound whirrs.
Black stand the ranks of its sentinel firs.

While I Slept

by Robert Francis

ABOUT THE SELECTION

Robert Francis (1901–1987) was born in Upland, Pennsylvania, earned two degrees at Harvard University, and became a professional writer of poetry, essays, fiction, and autobiography. His first collection of poetry was published in 1936; in 1939 he received the first of many awards for his writing. He was a friend of Robert Frost, who called Francis "the best neglected poet." In "While I Slept" Francis describes the sense of loss after the death of a loved one.

While I slept, while I slept and the night grew colder
She would come to my bedroom stepping softly
And draw a blanket about my shoulder
While I slept.

While I slept, while I slept in the dark still heat
She would come to my bedside stepping coolly
And smooth the twisted troubled sheet
While I slept.

Now she sleeps, sleeps under quiet rain
While nights grow warm or nights grow colder
And I wake and sleep and wake again
While she sleeps.

The Months

by Christina Rossetti

ABOUT THE SELECTION

English poet Christina Rossetti (1830–1894) was the sister of Dante Gabriel Rossetti, a famous poet and painter. Christina Rossetti was born in London and lived a sheltered life. Many of her poems deal with religious themes, but she also wrote a collection of poems for young children called *Sing-Song* (1872). "The Months" appears to be a simple verse for children, but if you read it aloud you will hear some surprises in it.

January desolate;[1]
February dripping wet;
March wind ranges;
April changes;
Birds sing in tune
To flowers of May
And sunny June
Brings longest day;
In scorched July
The storm-clouds fly
Lightning-torn;
August bears corn,
September fruit;
In rough October
Earth must disrobe her;
Stars fall and shoot
In keen November;
And night is long
And cold is strong
In bleak December.

---

[1] lifeless; dreary

Moon

by Myra Cohn Livingston

ABOUT THE SELECTION

Myra Cohn Livingston (1926–1996) was a poet and educator known for her work in children's literature. One of her major concerns was that modern children are losing their powers of imagination, and she encouraged children to write creatively. For more information about Livingston, see About This Poet at the beginning of this unit. "The Moon" comes from a collection entitled *Space Songs* (1988).

Moon remembers.

Marooned[1] in shadowed night,

white powder plastered
on her pockmarked[2] face,
scarred with craters,
filled with waterless seas,

she thinks back
to the Eagle,
to the flight
of men from Earth,
of rocks sent back in space,
and one
faint
footprint
in the Sea of Tranquility.

---

[1]abandoned, isolated

[2]covered with pitlike scars

Two Haiku

ABOUT THE SELECTIONS Muso Soseki (1275–1351) was an important religious leader in Japan. The haiku poem printed here was included in his single book of poetry. Kyorai (1651–1704) was the son of a physician who served a royal Japanese family. This sample of Kyorai's haiku suggests his concern for writing poems in which every word is essential.

Over the wintry
forest, winds howl in a rage
with no leaves to blow.
—by Soseki

I called to the wind,
"Who's there?" . . . Whoever it was
still knocks at my gate.
—by Kyorai

Limericks

Anonymous

ABOUT THE SELECTION

Limericks are rarely noted for such poetry elements as alliteration—the repetition of the same consonant sound or blend. "A flea and a fly in a flue," however, draws much of its humor from exaggerated alliteration. Whether Ryde is a real place or not is irrelevant to the enjoyment of the second limerick.

A flea and a fly in a flue[1]
Were caught, so what could they do?
   Said the fly, "Let us flee."
   "Let us fly," said the flea.
So they flew through a flaw in the flue.

---

[1] a pipe or tube for moving hot air, steam, gas, or smoke from one place to another, as from a fireplace to a chimney

There was once a young lady of Ryde
Who ate a green apple and died;
   The apple fermented[1]
   Inside the lamented,[2]
And made cider inside her inside.

---

[1] underwent a chemical reaction, particularly the conversion of sugar to carbon dioxide and alcohol

[2] one who is grieved or mourned

UNDERSTANDING THE POEMS

Record your answers to these questions in your personal literature notebook. Follow the directions for each group.

GROUP 1   Reread the poems in Group 1 to complete these sentences.

Reviewing the
Selections

1. In "The Months" the poet says that shooting stars can be seen in
   a. January.
   b. April.
   c. October.
   d. November.

2. The speaker in "When I Heard the Learn'd Astronomer" was
   a. taking a private class from an astronomer.
   b. talking with an astronomer at a social gathering.
   c. watching a program about astronomy on television.
   d. listening to an astronomer speak at a public lecture.

Interpreting the
Selection

3. The person being described in "While I Slept" is most likely the speaker's
   a. teacher.
   b. babysitter.
   c. mother.
   d. cousin.

Appreciating Poetry

4. The mood of "The Skater of Ghost Lake" can be described as
   a. humorous and playful.
   b. light and cheerful.
   c. biting and sarcastic.
   d. mysterious and frightening.

Recognizing How
Words Are Used

5. In "The Skater of Ghost Lake" the poet used such unfamiliar or made-up words as *flit-flit, skurr,* and *ring-tinkle-ring* because
  a. he simply enjoyed making up words.
  b. he wanted to make these words better known.
  c. their sounds suggest actions described in the poem.
  d. he wanted to confuse his readers.

GROUP 2   Reread the poems in Group 2 to complete these sentences.

Reviewing the
Selection

6. The message in the following poem indicates that it must have been written less than 40 years ago:
  a. "Moon"
  b. the haiku by Soseki
  c. "A Flea and a Fly"
  d. "There was once a young lady of Ryde"

7. The figure of speech used in "Moon" is
  a. a metaphor.
  b. a simile.
  c. personification.
  d. an idiom.

Interpreting the
Selection

8. The speaker in the haiku by Kyorai can best be described as
  a. so shy that he or she refuses to go to see who is at the gate.
  b. too lazy to go to see who is at the gate.
  c. imagining that the wind is a person knocking at the gate.
  d. angrily expecting whoever is at the gate to identify himself or herself.

Recognizing How Words Are Used

9. In "There was once a young lady of Ryde" the apple
   a. turned the lady's insides green.
   b. turned into apple cider in the lady's stomach.
   c. grew into a little apple tree in the lady's stomach.
   d. decomposed along with the lady's body.

Appreciating Poetry

10. Of the following poems the only one that does not use personification is
   a. "Moon."
   b. the haiku by Soseki.
   c. "A Flea and a Fly."
   d. "There was once a young lady of Ryde."

   Now check your answers with your teacher. Study the questions you answered incorrectly. What types of questions were they? Talk with your teacher about ways to work on those skills.

Form in Poetry

Every poem has a form, shape, or pattern of some kind. You can see a poem's visual form or shape when you read it on a page, and you can hear a poem's rhythmic pattern when you read it aloud. Sometimes a poem's visual form or sound pattern adds special meaning to the poem. You will gain a better appreciation of poems in general if you know what to look or listen for in their forms.

The lessons in this unit will explain some of the basic forms of poems and how those forms are written. The lessons will focus on these points:

- The forms of poems range from no particular form at all to very strict and stylized forms.
- Some forms of poetry are haiku, limericks, and concrete poems.

LESSON 1 | INTRODUCTION TO FORM

When many people hear the term *poetry*, they automatically think of rhyming verses with definite *meters*, or patterns of stressed and unstressed syllables. It is true that much poetry has rhyme and meter, but not every poem fits that description. The most important quality of poetry is that its language expresses ideas and experiences in a more powerful and imaginative way than normal language. The forms which that language can take are unlimited.

For hundreds of years, all English-speaking poets followed definite patterns of rhythm and rhyme. We often use the term *traditional* to describe such poetry. In the mid-1800s, however, a few poets—most notably Walt Whitman and other Americans—began to write poetry without definite forms. They felt that patterns limited them and that they could express themselves better in language that was free of rules. The poetry that they wrote is called *free verse*. Today, many poets write in free verse. Notice how much this passage of free verse from Whitman's "When I Heard the Learn'd Astronomer" sounds like normal speech:

> When I heard the learn'd astronomer,
> When the proofs, the figures, were ranged in columns
>   before me,
> When I was shown the charts and diagrams, to add,
>   divide, and measure them,
> When I sitting heard the astronomer where he lectured
>   with much applause in the lecture-room,

Each line is a different length. Each phrase follows a different pattern of stressed and unstressed syllables. There is no rhyme beyond the near rhyme of *heard* and *learn'd*. Except for a few words that seem to be in unusual positions, these lines sound like something you might hear someone say in a typical conversation.

By contrast, the poem "While I Slept" is not written in free verse. The lines are grouped in four-line stanzas, with the last line in every stanza having the same number of words. Also, the other three lines in each stanza correspond closely in length to the matching lines in the other stanzas. When you read the poem, you discover more patterns:

> ⏑ ⏑ / ⏑ ⏑ / ⏑ ⏑ / ⏑ / ⏑
> While I slept, while I slept and the night grew colder
> ⏑ ⏑ / ⏑ ⏑ / ⏑ / ⏑ / ⏑
> She would come to my bedroom stepping softly
> ⏑ / ⏑ / ⏑ ⏑ / ⏑ / ⏑
> And draw a blanket about my shoulder
> ⏑ ⏑ /
> While I slept.

Each of the marks for a stressed syllable indicates a measure called a *foot*. Although the arrangement of stressed and unstressed syllables is not totally regular in this stanza, each of its first three lines has four *feet*. The first and third lines also end in rhymes, while the first and fourth lines begin with the same phrase. The other stanzas in this poem have the same characteristics, except for a small variation in stanza 3.

This poem, therefore, has a distinctive form. It combines a characteristic of free verse—loose rhythm—with characteristics of traditional poetry—regular patterns of line lengths, rhyme, and repetition. The poet has chosen those elements of form that he feels best convey the poem's meaning and mood.

How does the form of "The Skater of Ghost Lake" contrast with that of "While I Slept"? Below, the first stanza of "The Skater" has been marked to show the stressed and unstressed syllables. Do you find a regular pattern of rhythm? After you examine this stanza, review other stanzas in the poem to see whether they match this one.

/ ∪ ∪ / ∪ ∪ / ∪ ∪ /
Ghost Lake's a dark lake, a deep lake and cold:
/ ∪ ∪ /∪∪ / ∪∪ /
Ice black as ebony, frostily scrolled;
/ ∪∪ / ∪ ∪ / ∪ /
Far in its shadows a faint sound whirrs;
/ ∪ ∪ / ∪∪ / ∪ /
Steep stand the sentineled deep, dark firs.

The steady rhythm of this poem contrasts sharply with the first two poems you examined. This poem has four feet in every line, just as "While I Slept" does. However, it is much more regular in the number of unstressed syllables per foot. This fairly strict pattern emphasizes the rhythmic movements of the skater, and the break in the middle of many lines even suggests the skater's switching from one foot to the other:

$$\text{|} \quad \overset{/}{\text{Ghost}} \; \overset{\cup}{\text{Lake's}} \; \overset{\cup}{\text{a}} \; \overset{/}{\text{dark}} \; \overset{\cup}{\text{lake,}} \qquad \overset{\cup}{\text{a}} \; \overset{/}{\text{deep}} \; \overset{\cup}{\text{lake}} \; \overset{\cup}{\text{and}} \; \overset{/}{\text{cold:}} \quad \text{|}$$

To the poet, the extra impact that this unusual rhythm gives the poem must have outweighed the difficulty of maintaining it over so many stanzas.

The four-line stanzas of the poem follow a simple *aabb* rhyme scheme. Because the lines are joined in "couples" by rhyme—for example, *cold/scrolled* and *whirrs/firs*—each pair of lines is called a *couplet*. This uncomplicated rhyme scheme doesn't interfere with the poem's intricate rhythm.

In many other poems with four-line stanzas, the rhyme scheme is somewhat more complex. All four lines are involved in one pattern, such as *abcb*, *abba*, or *abab*. Such four-line stanzas are called *quatrains*. Couplets and quatrains are both very popular forms of poetry.

When you read any poem, keep in mind that the poet had great freedom in choosing the poem's form. Determine what form he or she selected and consider possible reasons for that choice. How does the poem's particular form help express or emphasize its meaning? Examining its form will help you better understand and appreciate a poem.

EXERCISE ☐1☐

Reread the poems in Group 1. Then use what you have learned in this lesson to answer the following questions:

1. Copy the poem "The Months" onto a sheet of paper, leaving space above and below each line. Mark the stressed and unstressed syllables in the whole poem. (Hint: some of the lines begin with a stressed syllable followed by one or two unstressed syllables; other lines begin with an

unstressed syllable followed by a stressed one.) Where do you find changes from one metrical pattern to another?

2. Next, label the rhyme scheme throughout the entire poem. How does it change? Do the changes in rhyme scheme match the changes in metrical patterns?

3. Why do you suppose the poet changed the patterns of rhythm and rhyme within a single poem? How do the changes contribute to the meaning?

Now check your answers with your teacher. Review this part of the lesson if you don't understand why an answer was incorrect.

 WRITING ON YOUR OWN

Now that you are familiar with various elements of form, you will apply some of those forms in your own writing. Follow these steps:

• Recall a recent experience that brought out a strong emotional response in you, such as sorrow, joy, wonder, hilarity, or disgust. What parts of the experience would you need to tell others about in order to help them understand your reaction? Choose only a small number of details about the experience. Jot them down in the journal that you began in the first writing exercise.
• Write a free-verse poem of 12 lines or less.
• What form(s) can help express some aspect of your free-verse poem? If your poem is about a funny experience, rhyming double and triple syllables might stress the humor. If the poem is about a sad experience, perhaps a quatrain in slow and regular rhythm would be fitting. Rewrite your poem or some part of it as a poem with patterns of rhyme and rhythm.

LESSON 2 | THREE SPECIAL FORMS OF POETRY

There is only one rule for writing a couplet: the two lines must rhyme at the end. They can be of any length and follow any metrical pattern, however. Similarly, a quatrain has a limited choice of rhyme schemes but otherwise is open to all sorts of variations. Couplets and quatrains are used in poems about any subject. Other forms of poetry, however, are defined by stricter and more complex patterns. Frequently, poets discover that a particular form works well with a particular subject or range of subjects, and they tend to use the form only with those subjects. Three special forms of poetry are the concrete poem, the haiku, and the limerick.

Concrete poetry is poetry in which appearance is as important as language. A concrete poem may use patterns of rhyme and meter, or it may be in free verse. Either way, the arrangement of the written words helps to express the poem's meaning. The words are usually arranged to form a shape that suggests the subject of the poem. An example of a concrete poem is "Moon," whose words are arranged in the shape of a new moon.

Haiku is a form of poetry that has been adapted from Japanese poetry. Most haiku are made up of exactly seventeen syllables arranged in three lines, in a 5-7-5 pattern. (Sometimes translating a poem that was originally written in Japanese changes the number of syllables, so you may see some variations.) Here is an example of haiku:

> Over the wintry
> forest, winds howl in a rage
> with no leaves to blow.

A haiku poem focuses on something in nature, such as an animal or a force of nature, and suggests a season or a feeling. Notice how the haiku quoted here accomplishes both aims: we are told about the bareness of the trees in winter, and the personification of the wind suggests the emotion of anger.

A *limerick* is a humorous poem that has five lines in a specific pattern of rhythm and rhyme. Lines 1, 2, and 5 have three metrical feet; lines 3 and 4 have only two. The rhyme scheme is *aabba*. Often, the last word in line 1 is a place name. However, that rule is bent somewhat in the following example:

> A flea and a fly in a flue
> Were caught, so what could they do?
>   Said the fly, "Let us flee."
>   "Let us fly," said the flea.
> So they flew through a flaw in the flue.

Since limericks are often passed by word of mouth rather than written down, their authors are frequently unknown. As in the example above, limericks often involve plays on words. Unlike other poems, whose purpose is to call forth an emotional or thoughtful response in readers, limericks have only one purpose—to entertain.

EXERCISE 2

Reread the poems in Group 2. Then use what you have learned in this lesson to answer the following questions:

1. Compare the haiku by Kyorai to the requirements of haiku described in this lesson. Does the form of this haiku vary from the standard number and arrangement of syllables? If so, how? Does the content of this poem match the usual content of haiku poetry? Explain how the Kyorai poem does or does not match the description.

2. Which of the two limericks better satisfies the *aabba* rhyme scheme of limericks? Give a reason for your answer. Also, discuss alliteration in the limerick you chose.

Now check your answers with your teacher. Review this part of the lesson if you don't understand why an answer was incorrect.

 WRITING ON YOUR OWN 2

You are now familiar with the forms and characteristics of concrete poetry, haiku, and limericks. Now it's time to apply that knowledge to some poems that you write yourself. Follow these steps:

• Choose one of the following topics and write a concrete poem about it. Make sure that the shape of your poem reflects its topic: a hot dog, a train, a lightbulb, a computer screen, a book, a pizza.
• Review the requirements for haiku poetry. Choose one of the following topics and write a poem in haiku form about it: a spider, a butterfly, a flower, a rainstorm, snow, stars.
• Work with a partner to write a limerick that uses this as its first line: "There once was a creature from space." Be sure your limerick follows the traditional rhyme scheme and metrical pattern discussed in this lesson. Test your limerick on some classmates to see whether it gets a smile.

DISCUSSION GUIDES

1. Why does the speaker in "When I Heard the Learn'd Astronomer" need to leave the lecture room and go outside to see the stars? Does modern technology ever make you feel this way? Would it be a good idea for society to stop scientific research in order to avoid these feelings? Why or why not?

2. Which one of the poems in this unit brought forth the strongest emotional reaction in you? Did it make you feel good, or did it upset you? Why do you suppose it affected you that way? Was it some characteristic of the poem, something in your experience, or a combination of the two, that caused the reaction? Discuss this question with a small group and compare your reactions to the poems.

3. Imagine you are stranded on a desert isle. Which four poems in this unit would you like to have along with you? They need not be the most famous or the most complex poems, just the four that you'd enjoy most over a long period of time. Share your choices in a class discussion. Then take a poll to find out the class's favorite poems in this unit. Display the results in a bar graph, highlighting the class's first four choices.

4. Select one of the shorter poems in this unit and present it to someone in your family. Practice reading it aloud beforehand, and memorize it if possible. Afterward, report back to the class which element of the presentation or the poem your family member liked best. Considering the reaction you received, would you choose to present the same poem if you had it to do over? If not, which other poem would you choose? Why?

BEGIN A POETRY DICTIONARY

In this unit you have learned about several forms of poetry and their characteristics. You also have written poems using some of those forms, such as couplets, quatrains, concrete poems, haiku, and limericks. So as to remember what you've learned—and to use the information in the future—you will begin your own poetry dictionary. Follow these steps:

- Assemble the work you did for all the writing exercises in this unit: 1) a journal listing of ideas for poems and a list of formats in which writing can be communicated; 2) a poem in free verse and a traditional poem on the same topic; 3) a concrete poem, a haiku poem, and a limerick.
- Go back through your assignments and the pages of this unit and make a list of the forms and characteristics of poetry that you learned about. Your list should include some or all of the following: characteristics—*rhyme scheme, foot/feet, meter, repetition, couplet, quatrain;* forms—*free verse, concrete poem, haiku, limerick.*
- Rearrange the items on your list in alphabetical order, the way they will appear in your poetry dictionary.
- Using a separate sheet of paper for each entry in your dictionary, do the following: 1) Write the name of the characteristic or form of poetry at the top of the page, 2) write a definition or explanation of the characteristic or form, 3) write one or more examples of the characteristic or form. (Examples can come from the poems in this unit, or they can come from poems you have written.)
- When you have completed a page for each entry, share your work with a partner. If you or your partner is missing a particular entry, help each other create that page.
- Put your pages together into a booklet, adding a cover if you'd like. Keep your poetry dictionary with your writing journal or portfolio. Add new definitions and examples as you learn about them, and use your dictionary whenever you need ideas for writing poetry in the future.

Author's Purpose

Group 1

Hands
by Robinson Jeffers

Ancestors
by Dudley Randall

**And They Lived Happily Ever After
for a While**
by John Ciardi

Group 2

Almost Perfect
by Shel Silverstein

To My Dear and Loving Husband
by Anne Bradstreet

I Ask My Mother to Sing
by Li-Young Lee

Group 3

The Right Kind of People
by Edwin Markham

The Giveaway
by Phyllis McGinley

INTRODUCTION

ABOUT THE LESSONS

Poems are more than just their sounds, images, and formats. They are also an enjoyable and effective way for poets to share messages with readers. Through the messages in their poems, poets can entertain readers, teach them new things, share information, or persuade them to think or act a certain way. By sharing their attitudes toward different subjects, poets can move their readers to start thinking about and reacting to those subjects.

The first lesson in this unit focuses on the themes, or messages, found in poems. Lesson 2 explores the speaker's tone, or attitude, toward the subject of each poem. Lesson 3 shows you how to discuss and evaluate poems from your personal point of view.

 WRITING: DICUSSING A POEM

In this unit you will focus on certain elements of poetry that have only been touched upon lightly in other lessons—theme and tone. Using your understanding of theme, tone, and the many other elements of poetry, you will write a short essay at the end of this unit. In your essay you will discuss various ways of looking at a particular poem and why you would or wouldn't recommend it to friends. Follow these steps to begin thinking about the poems you could use in your essay:

- Look over the poems you have read so far in this book. In each unit, choose one or two of the poems you like best and write their titles on a list.
- Next to each poem on your list, write the reasons you chose it. Was it the use of rhyme or rhythm? Did you like the speaker or the message the poem conveyed? Did you

enjoy the images or the figurative language? Make and save notes on everything you remember and like about each poem. You will use them in later writing exercises.

ABOUT THIS POET

Shel Silverstein (1932–) was born Shelby Silverstein in Chicago, Illinois. During the 1950s, he served in the U.S. armed forces in Japan and Korea, and drew cartoons for the military publication *The Pacific Stars and Stripes.* When he returned to the United States after the Korean War, he became a staff cartoonist for a national magazine. During the 1960s he took up song writing. He composed a number of songs made popular by singers such as Johnny Cash ("A Boy Named Sue"), Lynn Anderson, the Irish Rovers ("The Unicorn"), the Brothers Four, and Jerry Lee Lewis. His song "Checkin' Out" won an Academy Award nomination for Best Song in 1991. His scores for motion pictures have also been well received.

Silverstein may be best known for his books of poetry for children, which have been popular for years. In them he speaks in a voice that children can relate to and enjoy. It seems that even though he is an adult, he has maintained an understanding of what it is like to be a child. He writes about ideas that are important or fascinating to children, and he never talks down to his young readers. His poems usually have a definite rhythm and rhyme and display a sly sense of humor. Although the poems are aimed at children, adults enjoy them too. During his live performances and the energetic recordings of his poems, he shows that he enjoys his own words as much as his listeners do.

His most popular children's books include *The Giving Tree, Falling Up,* and *The Missing Piece,* and the award-winning *Where the Sidewalk Ends, A Light in the Attic,* and The *Missing Piece Meets the Big* O. He also has written screenplays and stage plays.

Silverstein lives on a houseboat near Sausalito, California. He has chosen to live on a boat so he can travel anywhere he wants to at a moment's notice.

AS YOU READ   As you read each poem in this unit, ask these questions:

- For what purpose has the poet written this poem? What theme, or message, is the poet trying to send?
- What is the speaker's attitude in this poem?
- How would I go about analyzing this poem? What do I like or dislike about it? What has the poet done particularly well?

Hands

by Robinson Jeffers

ABOUT THE SELECTION

Robinson Jeffers (1887–1962) was born in Pittsburgh, Pennsylvania, but spent most of his life in California. He studied both medicine and forestry but decided that he would rather write poetry and plays than continue his studies. After his marriage he moved to Monterey, California, where he built his own home. In much of his writing, he expresses his appreciation for nature and his contempt for modern society. Read this poem to see whether he feels the same about the people who lived long ago.

Inside a cave in a narrow canyon near Tassajara
The vault of rock is painted with hands,
A multitude of hands in the twilight, a cloud of men's palms,
　　no more,
No other picture. There's no one to say
Whether the brown shy quiet people who are dead intended
Religion or magic, or made their tracings
In the idleness of art; but over the division of years these
　　careful
Signs-manual are now like a sealed message
Saying: "Look: we also were human; we had hands, not paws.
　　All hail
You people with the cleverer hands, our supplanters[1]
In the beautiful country; enjoy her a season, her beauty and
　　come down
And be supplanted; for you also are human."

---

[1] people who took the place of, or replaced, other people

207

Ancestors

by Dudley Randall

ABOUT THE SELECTION

Dudley Randall (1914–   ) is the founder of *Detroit's Broadside Press,* a publication that features the work of African-American poets. In 1981, Randall became the first poet laureate (best poet) of Detroit. The speaker in this poem expresses the same pride in his heritage that Randall himself seems to feel.

Why are our ancestors
always kings or princes
and never the common people?

Was the Old Country a democracy
where every man was a king?
Or did the slavecatchers
take only the aristocracy[1]
and leave the fieldhands
laborers
streetcleaners
garbage collectors
dishwashers
cooks
and maids
behind?

---

[1] upper class people; people thought to be superior

My own ancestor
(research reveals)
was a swineherd
who tended the pigs
in the Royal Pigstye
and slept in the mud
among the hogs.

Yet I'm as proud of him
as of any king or prince
dreamed up in fantasies
of bygone glory.

And They Lived Happily Ever After for a While

by John Ciardi

ABOUT THE SELECTION

John Ciardi (1916–1986) was born in Boston, Massachusetts. Ciardi wrote poetry for children and adults and lectured on poetry around the United States. In addition to writing poetry, he translated the Italian poet Dante's works into English. See About This Poet in Unit 4 for more information about John Ciardi. What do you think Ciardi's purpose was in writing this poem? What message was he trying to send?

It was down by the Dirty River
   As the Smog was beginning to thin
Because we had been so busy
   Breathing the worst of it in,

That the worst remained inside us
   And whatever we breathed back
Was only—sort of—grayish,
   Or at least not entirely black.

It was down by the Dirty River
   That flows to the Sticky Sea
I gave my heart to my Bonnie,
   And she gave hers to me.

I coughed: "I love you, Bonnie.
    And do you love me true?"
The tears of joy flowed from my eyes
    When she sneezed back: "Yes—Achoo!"

It was high in the Garbage Mountains,
    In Saint Snivens by the Scent,
I married my darling Bonnie
    And we built our Oxygen Tent.

And here till the tanks are empty
    We sit and watch TV
And dream of the Dirty River
    On its way to the Sticky Sea.

Here till the needles quiver
    Shut on the zero mark
We sit hand in hand while the TV screen
    Shines like a moon in the dark.

I cough: "I love you, Bonnie.
    And do you love me true?"
And tears of joy flow from our eyes
    When she sneezes: "Yes—Achoo!"

Almost Perfect

by Shel Silverstein

ABOUT THE SELECTION

Among other things, Shel Silverstein (1932–   ) is a cartoonist, songwriter, and poet. You may have read some of his poems in two of his most popular books of poetry, *Where the Sidewalk Ends* and *A Light in the Attic*. Many of his poems, including "Almost Perfect," display a light touch and a refreshing sense of humor. For more information about Silverstein, see About This Poet at the beginning of this unit.

"Almost perfect . . . but not quite."
Those were the words of Mary Hume
At her seventh birthday party,
Looking 'round the ribboned room.
"This tablecloth is *pink* not *white*—
Almost perfect . . . but not quite."

"Almost perfect . . . but not quite."
Those were the words of grown-up Mary
Talking about her handsome beau,
The one she wasn't gonna marry.
"Squeezes me a bit too tight—
Almost perfect . . . but not quite."

"Almost perfect . . . but not quite."
Those were the words of ol' Miss Hume
Teaching in the seventh grade,
Grading papers in the gloom
Late at night up in her room.
"They never cross their t's just right—
Almost perfect . . . but not quite."

Ninety-eight the day she died
Complainin' 'bout the spotless floor.
People shook their heads and sighed,
"Guess that she'll like heaven more."
Up went her soul on feathered wings,
Out the door, up out of sight.
Another voice from heaven came—
"Almost perfect . . . but not quite."

To My Dear and Loving Husband

by Anne Bradstreet

ABOUT THE SELECTION

Anne Bradstreet (1612–1672) was the first American woman poet to have her works published. She was born in England into a wealthy family and was well educated. At 16, Anne married Simon Bradstreet. A year later the couple sailed to the English colony of Massachusetts in North America. Simon Bradstreet eventually became the governor of Massachusetts. Although Anne was extremely busy bringing up eight children, she produced a 400-page book of poetry by 1650. Her book was published anonymously in London that year. Bradstreet continued writing until her death.

If ever two were one, then surely we.
If ever man were lov'd by wife, then thee;
If ever wife was happy in a man,
Compare with me ye women if you can.
I prize thy love more than whole mines of
    gold,
Or all the riches that the East doth hold.
My love is such that rivers cannot quench,
Nor aught but love from thee give recompence.
They love is such I can no way repay,
The heavens reward thee manifold I pray.
Then while we live, in love let's so persever,
That when we live no more, we may live ever.

I Ask My Mother to Sing

Li-Young Lee

ABOUT THE SELECTION

Li-Young Lee (1957–   ) was born into a Chinese family living in Jakarta, Indonesia. He moved with his parents to the United States when he was six years old. He attended the University of Pittsburgh, the University of Arizona, and the State University of New York at Brockport. This poem is from his award-winning first book of poetry, *Rose.*

She begins, and my grandmother joins her.
Mother and daughter sing like young girls.
If my father were alive, he would play
his accordion and sway like a boat.

I've never been in Peking, or the Summer Palace,
nor stood on the great Stone Boat to watch
the rain begin on Kuen Ming Lake, the picnickers
running away in the grass.

But I love to hear it sung;
how the waterlilies fill with rain until
they overturn, spilling water into water,
then rock back, and fill with more.

Both women have begun to cry.
But neither stops her song.

The Right Kind of People

by Edwin Markham

ABOUT THE SELECTION

Edwin Markham (1852–1940) was born Charles Edward Anson in Oregon City, Oregon. He became a teacher first, then a principal, and then a school superintendent in California. In 1899 he moved to New York, where he lectured and wrote poetry. In this poem he shares an insight about the best way to look at life.

Gone is the city, gone the day,
Yet still the story and the meaning stay:

Once where a prophet in the palm shade basked
A traveler chanced at noon to rest his miles.
"What sort of people may they be," he asked,
"In this proud city on the plains o'erspread?"
"Well, friend, what sort of people whence you came?"
"What sort?" the packman scowled, "why, knaves and fools."
"You'll find the people here the same," the wise man said.

Another stranger in the dusk drew near,
And pausing, cried, "What sort of people here
In your bright city where yon towers arise?"
"Well, friend, what sort of people whence you came?"
"What sort?" the pilgrim smiled.
"Good, true and wise."
"You'll find the people here the same,"
The wise man said.

The Giveaway

by Phyllis McGinley

ABOUT THE SELECTION

Phyllis McGinley (1905–1978), a prize-winning poet and writer of children's books, was widely praised as one of the most gifted writers of light verse of her time. She was born in Ontario, Oregon, attended college in the West, and began teaching in Utah. In 1929, when New York magazines began publishing her poems, she moved East and lived the rest of her life in or near New York City. McGinley wrote hundreds of lighthearted but skillful poems about suburbia, child rearing, commuting, and everyday life. "The Giveaway" tells the story of a patron saint of Ireland, which is referred to in the poem by one of its other names, the Isles of Erin. This poem is from *Times Three: Selected Verse from Three Decades*. In 1961 McGinley was awarded the Pulitzer Prize for poetry for this volume.

Saint Bridget was
A problem child.
Although a lass
Demure and mild,
And one who strove
To please her dad,
Saint Bridget drove
The family mad.
For here's the fault in Bridget lay
She *would* give everything away.

To any soul
Whose luck was out
She'd give her bowl
Of stirabout;
She'd give her shawl,
Divide her purse
With one or all.
And what was worse,
When she ran out of things to give
She'd borrow them from a relative.

Her father's gold,
Her grandsire's dinner,
She'd hand to cold
And hungry sinner;
Give wine, give meat,
No matter whose;
Take from her feet
The very shoes,
And when her shoes had gone to others,
Fetch forth her sister's and her mother's.

She could not quit.
She had to share;
Gave bit by bit
The silverware,
The barnyard geese,
The parlor rug,
Her little niece-
'S christening mug,
Even her bed to those in want,
And then the mattress of her aunt.

An easy touch
For poor and lowly,
She gave so much
And grew so holy
That when she died
Of years and fame,
The countryside
Put on her name,
And still the Isles of Erin fidget
With generous girls named Bride or Bridget.

Well, one must love her.
Nonetheless,
In thinking of her
Givingness,
There's no denial
She must have been
A sort of trial
To her kin.
The moral, too, seems rather quaint.
Who had the patience of a saint,
From evidence presented here?
Saint Bridget? Or her near and dear?

UNDERSTANDING THE POEMS
Record your answers to these questions in your personal literature notebook. Follow the directions for each group.

GROUP 1   Reread the poems in Group 1 to complete these sentences.

Reviewing the Selection

1. The cave painting described in "Hands" displays painted hands arranged in a
   a. horizontal line.
   b. circle.
   c. cloud shape.
   d. magical star shape.

2. In "Ancestor" the speaker's ancestor was a
   a. nobleman.
   b. swineherd.
   c. maid.
   d. slavecatcher.

Interpreting the Selection

3. The characters in "And They Lived Happily Ever After for a While" have trouble talking because
   a. the smog has affected their health.
   b. their love can't be put into words.
   c. they have nothing to say to each other.
   d. they are only pretending to like each other.

Recognizing How Words Are Used

4. In "And They Lived Happily Ever After for a While," the line "In Saint Snivens by the Scent" contains an example of
   a. rhyme
   b. alliteration
   c. assonance
   d. onomatopoeia

Appreciating Poetry

5. The mood of the poem "Hands" is
   a. joyful.
   b. exciting.
   c. angry.
   d. thoughtful.

GROUP 2   Reread the poems in Group 2 to complete these sentences.

Reviewing the Selection

6. In "Almost Perfect" the only thing that Mary Hume never complains is not quite perfect is
   a. the tablecloth at her party.
   b. her students' papers.
   c. herself.
   d. her boyfriend.

7. In "I Ask My Mother to Sing," the speaker says that if his father were alive he would
   a. stop his mother and grandmother from singing the song.
   b. sing along with his mother and grandmother.
   c. begin to cry when he heard the song.
   d. play his accordion along with the singing.

Interpreting the Selection

8. To emphasize that her love for her husband cannot die, the speaker in "To My Dear and Loving Husband" says
   a. "If ever two were one, then surely we."
   b. "My love is such that rivers cannot quench."
   c. "The heavens reward thee manifold I pray."
   d. Thy love is such I can no way repay."

Recognizing How Words Are Used

9. The rhyme scheme of the first two stanzas of "Almost Perfect" follows the pattern
   a. *abcbaa.*
   b. *aabbaa.*
   c. *abccaa.*
   d. *abccab.*

Appreciating Poetry **10.** After three four-line stanzas in "I Ask My Mother to Sing," the poet ends with a two-line stanza because he
a. is overcome with emotion.
b. runs out of room on the page.
c. wants those lines to stand out most.
d. can't think of anything else to say.

GROUP 3 Reread the poems in Group 3 to complete these sentences.

Reviewing the **11.** In "The Right Kind of People," the prophet predicts that
Selection the man who found the people in his old town foolish will find people in the new town
a. more intelligent.
b. foolish as well.
c. true and wise.
d. proud.

12. In the same poem, the prophet predicts that the traveler whose former town was filled with good people will find that the new town is filled with
a. fools and knaves.
b. prophets.
c. more good people.
d. hard workers.

Interpreting the **13.** The words of the prophet suggest that
Selection a. you can find whatever you look for in people.
b. most people are good, true, and wise.
c. travelers should stay in their own cities.
d. knaves and fools often live together.

Recognizing How **14.** The rhyme in the first four lines of each verse in "The
Words Are Used Giveaway" follows this rhyme scheme:
a. *aabb*
b. *abba*
c. *abcb*
d. *abab*

Appreciating Poetry   **15.** "The Giveaway" pays its highest tribute to
    a. Saint Bridget.
    b. people who name their children after Saint Bridget.
    c. Saint Bridget's family.
    d. the Isles of Erin.

Now check your answers with your teacher. Study the questions you answered incorrectly. What types of questions were they? Talk with your teacher about ways to work on those skills.

Author's Purpose

Every author or poet has a purpose in mind when he or she writes. Although the exact purpose of each piece of writing is unique, most purposes for writing can be grouped into these major categories: to teach or inform, to entertain, to persuade, and to share feelings. Often a writer has more than one purpose for writing. For example, a poem may make you laugh as it teaches you a lesson.

In most poems, one of the author's goals is to convey a *theme*, or message about life. Themes can be communicated in a variety of ways. One of those ways is through the *tone*, or attitude, of the poem's speaker.

In the following lessons you will look at the themes and tones of a variety of poems. You also will learn how to discuss poems knowledgeably. The lessons will discuss these ideas:

- Sometimes a poet clearly states his or her theme. More often, however, readers must figure out the theme by what the speaker of a poem says.
- Poets influence the thinking and attitudes of their readers through the tone of their poems.
- Readers bring their own opinions and understandings to a poem and decide what it means to them personally.

LESSON 1 | AUTHOR'S PURPOSE AND THEME

No matter what authors write—short stories, novels, non-fiction, or poetry—they write for a purpose. As you learned earlier, this purpose can be simply to entertain or to share a feeling, but it also may be to persuade or to teach. For many authors, the goal in writing is to share a message, or theme, about life.

In a novel the theme may come up over and over throughout the course of the story. The novel writer has many opportunities to explain and expand upon that theme. However, in a poem—which is much shorter than a novel—the poet must present the theme quickly and strongly. Sometimes a complex theme is compressed into just a few short words, so it takes careful reading to understand the message that the poet is presenting.

For example, in "Hands" the speaker sees an ancient cave whose walls bear the imprint of a great number of human hands. The sight of the hands starts the speaker thinking about the people who placed their hands there so many years ago. The speaker feels a connection to the ancient people and tries to imagine what they were trying to say to their descendants:

> Saying: "Look: we also were human; he had hands, not paws.
> All hail.
> You people with the cleverer hands, our supplanters
> In the beautiful country; enjoy her a season, her beauty and come down
> And be supplanted; for you also are human."

In these few words, the speaker explains that he or she feels close to the ancient people. He or she also suggests that no matter how clever we think we are, we live for only "a season" upon the earth. Like the people who placed their handprints on the wall, we are destined to be replaced by those who come after us. We see that in all the centuries of their existence, human beings have not changed much after all.

"Hands" teaches an important lesson and discusses it in a respectful way. In contrast, "And They Lived Happily Ever After for a While" teaches just as important a lesson but in a lighter, more humorous way. What does the speaker in this poem see for the future of the human race?

And here till the tanks are empty
   We sit and watch TV
And dream of the Dirty River
   On its way to the Sticky Sea.

Here till the needles quiver
   Shut on the zero mark
We sit hand in hand while the TV screen
   Shines like a moon in the dark.

This speaker pictures a future in which the water and air are so polluted that all human beings will be able to do is sit and hope that their oxygen tanks won't run out. The speaker is warning us—in an ironically humorous way—that unless we preserve our environment, our futures will be bleak indeed.

EXERCISE 1

Reread "Ancestors" by Dudley Randall. Then use what you have learned in this lesson to answer the following questions:

1. What practice is the speaker complaining about at the beginning of this poem? Why does the speaker find that practice illogical and wrong?

2. Why is the speaker proud of his or her ancestor? Do you think you would feel the same way if you found that your ancestors did simple work and were not members of royalty? Why or why not?

Now check your answers with your teacher. Review this part of the lesson if you don't understand why an answer was incorrect.

WRITING ON YOUR OWN 1

In the first writing exercise, you chose your favorite poems in this book and gave reasons for your choices. Now you will focus on one aspect of one of those poems. Follow these steps:

- Look over your list of favorite poems and choose the ones that you think have clear themes. Record their titles in a new list. Don't forget to add poems from this unit that have clear themes too.
- Now read your new list of poems. Choose the one poem whose theme you agree with most strongly.
- Write one or two sentences explaining the theme. Then write another sentence telling why you agree with it.

LESSON 2   TONE

Meanings are communicated by more than just words. The tone of a speaker's voice is often just as important as the words he or she is saying. For example, if someone says "I can hardly wait" with a sincere, excited tone, his or her meaning seems sincere. However, if someone says the same words with a sarcastic tone, the meaning changes entirely. One tone conveys the true meaning of the words; the other tone conveys the opposite.

Tone, the writer's attitude toward the topic or the reader, is also important in poetry. It is more difficult to communicate, however, because the poet's voice cannot be heard. To create a clear tone, the poet must be sure that the speaker's voice and feelings are unmistakable.

Often the speaker of a poem exaggerates his or her attitude toward the subject or the reader. For example, in "Almost Perfect" the speaker happily relates the story of Mary Hume, who can find fault in just about everything.

Such a character trait leads Mary to a lonely life without love or satisfaction, but the speaker doesn't seem to care. In fact, the speaker seems to get some satisfaction when Mary, the faultfinder, gets what she deserves:

> Ninety-eight the day she died
> Complainin' 'bout the spotless floor.
> People shook their heads and sighed,
> "Guess that she'll like heaven more."
> Up went her soul on feathered wings,
> Out the door, up out of sight.
> Another voice from heaven came—
> "Almost perfect . . . but not quite."

Clearly, Mary does not measure up to the standards of heaven. Where will she be sent? We don't know and we don't care. We have adopted the exaggerated tone of the speaker, and we think it is funny and appropriate that Mary is judged to be imperfect, just as she judged others throughout her life. If we were looking for a theme in this poem we might say, "Accept the imperfections of life and you will be much happier."

While the speaker in "Almost Perfect" was flip and casual, the speaker in "I Ask My Mother to Sing" is much more serious and sad. You feel the speaker's sorrow while describing his or her mother and grandmother singing:

> She begins, and my grandmother joins her.
> Mother and daughter sing like young girls.
> If my father were alive, he would play
> his accordion and sway like a boat.

From these few words we understand the singers' longing and sadness, and we recognize that the tone of the speaker is loving and respectful. We take our cue from the speaker, and we honor the simple sincerity of the singers. Perhaps we extend that feeling to our own parents and others who miss their homeland and former way of life.

EXERCISE 2

Reread "To My Dear and Loving Husband." Then use what you have learned in this lesson to answer the questions below.

1. How would you describe the speaker's tone in this poem? To answer this question, think about how the speaker feels toward her husband. How is the speaker's tone in this poem similar to that of the speaker in "I Ask My Mother to Sing"? How is it different?

2. Why might the poet have written this poem? What might her purpose have been?

Now check your answers with your teacher. Review this part of the lesson if you don't understand why an answer was incorrect.

WRITING ON YOUR OWN 2

In this lesson you have explored some of the different tones that poems may have. Now you will write a paragraph with a particular kind of tone. Follow these steps:

- A poem can be written with any of the tones in which a person can speak—from funny to sarcastic to serious to angry. Choose a topic to write about from the list below. Then choose a tone for your paragraph.

Topics	Tones
parents	loving
family	critical
food	humorous
music	serious
school	friendly

- Write your paragraph, using the topic and the tone you have chosen. Begin with a sentence that introduces the topic and immediately establishes your tone.
- Let a classmate read your paragraph. Then see whether he or she can use the lists to identify your topic and tone. If necessary, make changes to your paragraph to make the topic clearer or the tone stronger.

LESSON 3

DISCUSSING POETRY

Not everyone likes every poem. Some poems that you read will mean a great deal to you, and you will remember them for years. Other poems will not mean much to you, and you will forget them right away. Just because you don't like a poem, however, doesn't mean that it is inferior. It may simply have qualities that you don't value or a message that you don't understand. Perhaps if you reread the poem in a few years, you will find that you appreciate it more.

Throughout this book you have been learning about the elements that make a good poem. You have explored the importance of the speaker, as well as images, sounds, figurative language, structure, theme, and tone. Armed with this knowledge of poetry, you now should be able to look at a poem and discuss its strengths and weaknesses.

When you discuss a poem, you do not need to analyze every aspect of it. However, you need to look at enough qualities of the poem to show that you have studied it thoroughly. Read the following discussion of "The Right Kind of People." Which elements of poetry does the writer discuss when he or she analyzes this poem?

"The Right Kind of People" by Edwin Markham teaches an important lesson about the power we have over our own lives. The poem tells the story of a wise man and two travelers. Both travelers ask the wise man what kind of people live in the city below. The wise man answers with another question, "What kind of people were there in the place you came from?" The travelers' replies to that question are very different.

The theme of this poem is that people often live up to our expectations of them. This theme makes a great deal of sense to me. The poem teaches me that whatever we expect from people is what they will give us. If we expect dishonesty, that is what we will see in people. If we expect kindness, we are more likely to find that people are kind.

I like the way this poem is written as a story from long ago. It begins with two lines that rhyme and get readers ready for a very old story. Each of the first two lines has four strong beats. Once the story begins, however, the number of strong beats in each line changes to five. The steady meter and the unusual order of the words makes the poem's story seem old and important.

The people in the poem speak as if they were from the old times too. They use words such as *whence* and *o'erspread*. These words take the story away from everyday life and into a kind of fairy-tale world.

I can see why this poem has become popular. Its use of words, its sounds, and its theme make it a poem worth reading.

The writer of this essay has given evidence from the poem to back up his or her opinions. After reading this essay, you know that the writer values the poem for its interesting story, its theme, the way the poem sounds, and the specific words that the poet has chosen to make the story seem old.

EXERCISE 3

Reread the poems in Group 3. Then use what you have learned in this lesson to answer the following questions.

1. Which of these elements of poetry would you be likely to concentrate on if you were to write about the poem "The Giveaway"? Explain why you chose each element.

   a. theme
   b. images
   c. figurative language
   d. speaker

   e. structure
   f. mood
   g. tone

2. Which of the poems in Group 3 would you recommend to a friend? to a young child? to an adult? For each recommendation, use evidence from the poem to explain why you chose it.

Now check your answers with your teacher. Review this part of the lesson if you don't understand why an answer was incorrect.

 WRITING ON YOUR OWN 3

In this exercise you will write a paragraph or poem explaining why you like a certain kind of poem. Follow these steps:

- Which kinds of poems do you like better: narrative poems that tell stories or ones in which poets share personal insights? Review poems in this book that fit each category and decide which kind you prefer. Then jot down some of the reasons you like a particular kind of poem.
- Next, decide how you want to explain your point of view—in a paragraph or in a poem. If you feel more comfortable writing in prose, write one or two paragraphs explaining your point of view. If you'd like to try something new, explain your opinion in a poem.

DISCUSSION GUIDES

1. In "The Giveaway" Phyllis McGinley describes the life of Saint Bridget, one of the saints of the Roman Catholic Church. There are hundreds of other saints honored by Roman Catholics. Each saint is known for certain good works, and some saints have been designated as the patrons of particular causes. Together with a partner do some research on various saints in the Catholic Church or on people who have been recognized as holy people in other faiths. Find the answers to questions such as the following: Why was this person considered to be holy? What was the person's life like? Present your research findings to the rest of your class.

2. Work with two or three classmates to make a collection of your favorite poems. The poems can be from this book, or they can be brought in from other sources. Each time you feel you have found a poem to include in your collection, read it aloud to the group. Then tell group members what you like best about the poem. Listen to their opinions about it and then decide together whether the poem should be included or not. Gather all the poems you have chosen and share them with your friends and family.

3. At the end of Unit 1, your class developed a questionnaire about your attitudes toward poetry. Now, take a few moments to answer the survey questions again. After the results are tabulated, see whether your class's attitudes toward poetry have changed. Then discuss how and why your attitudes have or have not changed.

WRITE AN ESSAY ABOUT A POEM

In this unit you have learned about the purposes, themes, and tones of poems. You also have learned how to evaluate poems. Now you will use what you have learned to write a short essay about a poem.

Follow these steps to write your essay. If you have questions about the writing process, refer to Using the Writing Process, which begins on the next page.

- Assemble the work you did for all the writing exercises in this unit: 1) a list of your favorite poems in this book and what you like best about them, 2) a statement of the theme of a poem, 3) a paragraph with a particular tone, 4) a paragraph or poem that explains why you like one kind of poem better than another.
- After you look over your list of favorite poems, choose the poem about which you have the most to say. Make sure you can focus on more than one element of the poem in your essay. Possible elements include the poem's speaker, images, sound devices, figurative language, mood, theme, tone, and choice of words. List the main elements that you hope to cover in your essay.
- Using your notes as a guide, write your first draft. Begin with a sentence that introduces readers to your topic and reveals your point of view. Then discuss the elements of the poem that you especially enjoyed or appreciated. Include as much supporting evidence from the poem as possible.
- End your essay with a brief statement about why you recommend the poem and to whom you recommend it.
- Proofread your essay for spelling, grammar, punctuation, capitalization, and formatting errors. Then make a final copy and read it to a group of your classmates. When you are finished, save your essay in your writing portfolio.

USING THE WRITING PROCESS

This reference section explains the major steps in the writing process. It will help you complete the writing exercises in this book. Read the information carefully so you can understand the process thoroughly. Whenever you need a quick review of important things to think about when you write, refer to the handy checklist on page 241.

Most tasks worth doing have several steps. For example, houses can be built only after the builder follows a number of complicated, logical steps. Moviemakers must go through a series of steps before releasing a film. Even a task as simple as making a peanut butter and jelly sandwich requires that the sandwich maker perform specific steps in order. So it should be no surprise that anyone who wants to write a good story, play, poem, report, or article must follow certain steps too. Taken together, the steps a writer follows are called the *writing process*. This writing process is divided into three main stages: prewriting, writing, and revising. Each stage is important for good writing.

STAGE 1: Prewriting

Prewriting consists of all the preparation you do before you put a single word down on paper. There are many decisions that you must make in order to make your writing as interesting, logical, and easy to read as possible. Here are the steps you should take before you begin to write:

1. **Decide on your audience.** Who will read your writing? Will your audience be your teacher? Will it be readers of the school newspaper? Or will your audience be family or friends? Your writing will change, depending on who you think your audience will be.

2. **Decide on your purpose.** Why are you writing? Do you want to teach your audience something? Do you want to entertain

them? Do you want to change someone's mind about an issue? Think about your purpose before you begin to write.

3. **Think about possible topics.** What are some topics that interest you? Make a list of topics that you are familiar with and might like to write about. Make another list of topics that interest you and that you want to learn about.

   One technique that helps some writers at this stage is *brainstorming.* When you brainstorm, you let your mind wander freely. Without judging your ideas first, scribble them down as they come to you—even if they seem silly or farfetched. Good ideas often develop from unusual thoughts.

   If you're having trouble coming up with ideas by yourself, brainstorm with a partner or a group of classmates. Jot down everyone's ideas as they say them. Brainstorming alone or with others should give you a long list of possible writing topics.

4. **Choose and narrow your topic.** Once you have chosen a topic, you will probably find that it is impossible to cover every aspect of it in one piece of writing. Say, for example, you have chosen to write about the possibility of life on other planets. In a single piece, you could not possibly include everything that has been researched about extraterrestrial life. Therefore, you must choose one or two aspects to focus on, such as alleged sightings in the United States or worldwide organizations that study extraterrestrial life. Otherwise, you might overload your writing with too many ideas. Concentrate on telling about a few things thoroughly and well.

5. **Research your topic.** You probably have had experience using an encyclopedia, the library, or the Internet to look up information for factual reports. Even when you write fictional stories, however, you often need to do some research. In a story set during the Civil War, for example, your characters

wouldn't use pocket cameras or wear suits of armor. In order to make your story as accurate and believable as possible, you would have to research how Americans lived and dressed during the years of the Civil War.

To conduct your research, you may want to use books, magazines, newspapers, reference works, or electronic sources. Some topics may require you to interview knowledgeable people. For realistic stories set in the present time, you may find that the best research is simple observation of everyday life. Thorough research will help ensure that your facts and details are accurate.

6. **Organize your research.** Once you have the facts, ideas, and details, you need to decide how to arrange them. Which order will you choose? No matter what you are writing, it is always helpful to begin with a written plan. If you are writing a story, you probably will tell it in time order. Make a list of the major story events, arranged from first to last.

Arranging details in time order is not the only way to organize information, however. Some writers start by making *lists* (informal outlines) of the facts and ideas they have gathered. Then they rearrange the items on their lists until they have the order that will work well in their writing.

Other writers make formal *outlines,* designating the most important ideas with roman numerals (I, II, III, IV, and so on) and related details with letters and numerals (A, B, C; 1, 2, 3; a, b, c; and so on). An outline is a more formal version of a list, and like the items in a list, the items in an outline can be rearranged until you decide on a logical order. Both outlines and lists help you organize and group your ideas.

Mapping or *clustering* is another helpful technique used by many writers. With this method, you write a main idea in the center of a cluster and then surround it with facts and ideas connected to that idea. Following is an example of a cluster map:

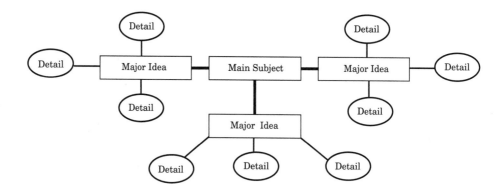

STAGE 2: Writing

1. **Get started.** Begin your writing with an introductory sentence or paragraph. A good introduction can become a guide for the rest of your piece. For ideas on good opening sentences, take a look at some of your favorite stories or magazine articles.

   Your introduction should give your audience a hint about what is coming next. If you are writing a story, your introduction should set the tone and mood. It should reveal the narrator's point of view, and it may introduce the main characters, the setting, and your purpose for writing. Do the best you can with your introduction, but remember that, if you wish to, you can always change it later.

2. **Keep writing.** Get your thoughts down as quickly as possible, referring to your prewriting notes to keep you on track. Later, when you are done with this *rough draft,* you will have a chance to revise and polish your work to make it as clear and accurate as possible. For right now, however, don't stop for spelling, grammar, or exact-wording problems. Come as close as you can to what you want to say but don't let yourself get bogged down in details.

STAGE 3: Revising

Now you're ready to revise your work. Careful revision includes editing and reorganizing that can make a big difference in the final product. You may wish to ask for suggestions from your classmates or your teacher about how to revise your work.

1. **Revise and edit your work.** When you are revising and editing, ask yourself these questions:
   - *Did I follow my prewriting plan?* Reread your entire first draft. Compare it to your original plan. Did you skip anything important? If you added an idea, did it work logically with the rest of your plan? Even if you decide that your prewriting plan is no longer what you want, it may include ideas you don't want to lose.
   - *Is my writing clear and logical?* Does one idea follow the other in a sensible order? Do you want to change the order or add ideas to make the organization clearer?
   - *Is my language clear and interesting?* Have you chosen exact verbs, nouns, and adjectives? For example, have you used forms of the verb *to be (is, are, being, become)* more often than you should? If so, replace them or change your sentence to make them unnecessary. Include precise action words such as *raced, hiked, zoomed,* and *hurried* in place of the overused verb *went.* Instead of using vague nouns such as *water* and *green,* choose exact ones such as *cascade* or *pond* and *lime.* Replace common adjectives such as *beautiful* and *nice* with precise ones such as *elegant, gorgeous,* and *lovely.*
   - *Is my writing clear and to the point?* Take out words that repeat the same ideas. For example, don't use both *liberty* and *freedom.* These words are synonyms. Choose one word or the other.

2. **Proofread for errors in spelling, grammar, capitalization, and punctuation.** Anyone reading your writing will notice such

errors immediately. These errors can confuse your readers or make them lose interest in what they are reading.

If you are in doubt about the spelling of a word, look it up or ask someone for help. If you are unsure about your grammar, read your writing aloud and listen carefully. Does anything sound wrong? Check with a friend or classmate if you need a second opinion—or refer to a grammar hand-book.

Make sure every group of words is a complete sentence. Are any of your sentences run-ons? Do proper nouns begin with capital letters? Is the first word of every sentence capi-talized? Do all your sentences have the correct end marks? Should you add any other punctuation to your writing to make your ideas even clearer? If your writing includes dia-logue, have you used quotation marks correctly?

3. **Make a clean final draft to share.** After you are satisfied with your writing, it is time to share it with your audience. If you are lucky enough to be composing on a computer, you can print out a final copy easily, after running a spell-check. If you are writing your final draft by hand, make sure your handwriting is clear and easy to read. Leave margins on both sides of the page. You may want to skip every other line. Make your writing look inviting to your readers. After all, you put a lot of work into this piece. It's important that someone read and enjoy it.

A WRITING CHECKLIST

Ask yourself these questions before beginning a writing assignment:

- Have I chosen a topic that is both interesting and manageable? Should I narrow it so I can cover it in the space that I have?
- Do I have a clear prewriting plan?
- What should I do to gather my facts and ideas? read? interview? observe?
- How will I organize my ideas? a list? an outline? a cluster map?
- Do I have an opening sentence or paragraph that will pull my readers in?
- Do I need to add more information? Switch the order of paragraphs? Take out unnecessary information?

Ask yourself these questions after completing a writing assignment:

- Did I use my prewriting plan?
- Is the organization of my writing clear? Should I move, add, or delete any paragraphs or sentences to make the ideas flow more logically?
- Do all the sentences in one paragraph relate to one idea?
- Have I used active, precise words? Is my language interesting? Do the words say what I mean to say?
- Are all the words spelled correctly?
- Have I used correct grammar, capitalization, punctuation, and formatting?
- Is my final draft legible, clean, and attractive?

GLOSSARY OF LITERARY TERMS

This glossary includes definitions for important literary terms that are introduced in this book. Boldfaced words within the definitions are other terms that appear in the glossary.

alliteration   the repetition of the same sounds within words that are close together. These sounds are usually consonant sounds that occur at the beginnings of words, but they also can occur within words.

assonance   the repetition of vowel sounds within words.

cliché   an overused phrase or expression.

concrete language   words and phrases that describe things that readers can experience with their senses. *See* **image** and **sensory detail**.

concrete poem   a poem whose shape resembles the object it describes. This shape helps contribute to the meaning of the poem.

connotation   the emotion that a word arouses or the meaning it suggests beyond its **denotation,** or dictionary meaning.

couplet   a pair of lines that rhyme.

denotation   the literal, dictionary meaning of a word.

dialect   a version of a language spoken in one place or time, by one group of people.

dialogue   a conversation between two characters.

end rhyme   rhyme that occurs at the ends of lines of poetry.

extended metaphor   a special kind of metaphor that involves the entire poem. The individual metaphors within the poem contribute directly to the main metaphor. *See* **figure of speech, figurative language, metaphor,** and **implied metaphor.**

figurative language   words and phrases used in such as way as to suggest something more than just their usual, dictionary meanings. *See* **figure of speech.**

figure of speech a word or phrase that suggests meanings other than the usual, dictionary meaning. Most figures of speech involve comparisons. Some figures of speech are simile, metaphor, hyperbole, and personification.

foot the unit in which meter is measured. A foot consists of one stressed syllable and one or more unstressed syllables. The number of feet in a line of poetry equals the number of stressed syllables. *See* **scanning** and **stress.**

free verse poetry that does not have fixed rhythm, rhyme, meter, or line length. A poet using free verse is free to change patterns or to use no pattern at all.

haiku a 3-line poem with 17 syllables. The first and third lines have 5 syllables each, and the second line has 7 syllables. The haiku, created first in Japan, expresses an experience by presenting one striking image.

hyperbole a figure of speech that exaggerates the truth to emphasize an idea or feeling. *See* **figurative language.**

imagery all the images that are created in a poem. *See* **sensory detail** and **sensory image**.

implied metaphor a kind of metaphor, also called *implicit metaphor,* in which one of the things being compared is not directly stated but is suggested by the context. "The shoppers swarmed into the store as soon as the doors opened" is an example of an implied metaphor in which the shoppers are indirectly compared to bees by the use of the word *swarmed. See* **figure of speech, figurative language, extended metaphor,** and **implied metaphor.**

limerick a short, humorous poem with five lines. Lines one, two, and five have three metric feet and lines three and four have two feet. The rhyme scheme is *aabba.*

lyric poem a poem that has a single speaker and expresses a deeply felt thought or emotion. Lyric poems have a musical quality. Often in a lyric poem, the speaker does not have a specific audience, but instead is addressing himself or herself.

metaphor   a figure of speech in which one thing is spoken about as if it were another, unlike thing. A metaphor helps readers *see* the similarities between these two things. *See* **figurative language, extended metaphor,** and **implied metaphor.**

meter   the regular rhythmic pattern of stressed and unstressed syllables in a line of poetry. Meter is counted in feet. *See* **foot** and **stress.**

monologue   a poem in which only one speaker talks.

mood   the general feeling or atmosphere created in a poem.

narrative poem   a poem that tells a story.

narrator   the speaker who tells the story in a narrative poem.

near-rhyme   a sound technique in which words with matching consonant sounds (**consonance**) or matching vowel sounds (**assonance**) are substituted for true rhymes, as in these word pairs: **wind/end** and **boat/hope.**

onomatopoeia   the use of words whose sounds imitate or suggest their meanings. Examples: *crash, buzz,* and *hiss.*

persona   the character who speaks in a poem. The poet speaks to the reader using that character's voice. *See* **speaker.**

personification   a figure of speech in which an animal, an object, or an idea is given human qualities. *See* **figurative language.**

point of view   vantage point from which a poem is written or a story is told. In a piece of literature written from a first-person point of view, the speaker uses words such as *I, me,* and *we.* In a piece written from the third-person point of view, the speaker uses the words *he, she,* and *they.*

prose   the ordinary form of written or spoken language, without any rhyme or regular rhythm. Short stories, novels, and essays are written in prose.

quatrain   a four-line stanza in a poem.

refrain   one or more lines that are repeated in a poem or a song.

repetition   the use of a sound, word, phrase, line, or stanza two or more times in a poem. *See* **refrain**.

rhyme   the repetition of ending sounds in two or more words. *See* **end rhyme,** and **near-rhyme**.

rhyme scheme   the pattern of end rhyme in a poem. The rhyme scheme can be determined if words at the ends of two or more lines rhyme. The rhyme scheme is shown by assigning a different letter of the alphabet to each line-end sound in a stanza. Lines that rhyme are given the same letter. For example, if the first and third lines rhyme and the second and fourth lines rhyme, the rhyme scheme is *abab*.

rhythm   the pattern of stressed and unstressed syllables in a poem. *See* **stress**.

scanning   counting the feet, or number and arrangement of stressed and unstressed syllables in a line, to determine the meter. *See* **foot** and **stress**.

sensory detail   a word or phrase that describes the way things look, sound, taste, smell, or feel. Sensory details are used to create **sensory images.**

sensory image   a mental picture created with words or phrases. Images can appeal to any of the senses—sight, hearing, taste, smell, and touch. Some images appeal to more than one sense.

setting   the time or place of the action in a poem or a story.

simile   a figure of speech that compares two unlike things, using the word *like, as, appear,* or *seem. See* **figurative language**.

sonnet   a fourteen-line poem with a fixed pattern of rhythm and meter that follows one of several rhyme schemes. A Shakespearean sonnet has four parts—three **quatrains** and a **couplet** at the end. Its rhyme scheme is *abab cdcd efef gg.*

speaker   the voice that speaks in a poem. The speaker may or may not be the poet. Often the poet assumes a **persona,** or alternate identity. *See* **narrator**.

stanza   a group of lines in a poem. Each stanza in a rhyming poem often has the same rhyme scheme. *See* **quatrain**.

stress   the emphasis given to a word or syllable. A strongly stressed syllable is marked with a straight line (/) and an unstressed syllable is marked with a curved line (∪), as in this example:

/ ∪   / ∪ /∪ /

Twinkle, twinkle, little star

structure   the overall design of a work. Structure refers to the way a poet arranges words, lines, and ideas to produce a particular effect.

symbol   a person, place, or thing that stands for something else.

theme   the insight or message that an author conveys in a piece of writing.

tone   a writer's attitude toward his or her subject, audience, or self.